MW01031884

Earth,

the Cosmos

and You

Revelations by Archangel Michael

Earth, the Cosmos and You

Revelations by Archangel Michael

Orpheus Phylos
and Virginia Essene

 S.E.E. Publishing Company, Santa Clara, California, USA

Spiritual Education Endeavors
Publishing Company
1556 Halford Avenue, #288
Santa Clara, CA 95051-2661 USA
Tel. (408) 245-5457

Orpheus' Dedication

I dedicate this book to the supreme "Oneness"—the life force that is the eternal breath that resides in every one of us, to all the beautiful celestials who protect and guide us, and to my divine council who made this possible. May we let go of prejudices, hatred and judgments in order to unite in bringing peace among all people and nations.

Orpheus Phylos

Virginia's Dedication

This ninth book in our series of publications is dedicated to the Creator of our souls, to Archangel Michael—and all angels—to Christ Jesus, Mother Mary, the Ascended Masters, and every teacher and guide who has helped us in our evolutionary journey. To these Masters of Love and our many cosmic helpers in the vast dimensions of creation, I give you my eternal gratitude!

I also wish to dedicate this book to all of my brothers and sisters on Earth who are awakening to their spiritual essence and who lovingly model their sacred commitments to all life.

Virginia Essene

Orpheus' Acknowledgments

There have been so many wonderful people who have contributed in helping me to accomplish this book and who have touched my life in ways mere words cannot express. At this time, I especially want to thank Toni, my twin ray, for her continuous support, unconditional love, and the incredible insight she offers to help keep me focused through my daily walk of life. I also acknowledge her husband Bob for helping me through some difficult times. My heart swells with gratitude for the unending love of Leonard and Linda and the enormous contribution of support and love that was given for my physical, emotional and spiritual well-being. I wish to acknowledge my son Geoff, who I am so proud of for his many accomplishments. It's his love, support, will power and strength that have given me the courage to get through some difficult times and to write this book. I also want to thank my beautiful daughter, Delanie, for being forthright, honest, and for offering practical criticism. She has always been by my side when I needed a hand to hold saying, "I love you, Mom!"

I wish to thank Vera and Walter for their hospitality in giving me a place to stay in California while finishing this book and to Vera for the time given in interviewing me and writing my introduction. I also want to thank Walter for drawing the graphic of the energy rods.

I want to especially thank my mother, who has passed on, but who was always there for me as my mentor, friend and confidant. She always listened to me and never put down my strange occurrences or prophetic visions. She would just say, "It's okay honey. Let's just wait and see what happens." Our souls are interlaced for eternity!

To Mina and Theresa, my soul sisters, for loving me and always being there, giving me support and hugs.

I want to acknowledge Virginia, who had the persistence to keep asking me to do this book until I finally said yes.

She had confidence in my ability and my work with the Archangel Michael, and loved me enough to support this endeavor with patience, insight and incredible devotion. Thank you for making my dream come true by following your inner voice! I also wish to thank Alma for her loving presence, devotion and her work in helping to put this book together. With great appreciation, I want to thank my cosmic family here on earth for their support and incredible love. Allan, Sheila, Bob, Bill, Bobbie, Elizabeth, Kathy, Geoff, Alan, Gene, Ruby, Pam and the Rose Garden. Also, Irene, Katherine, Rayne, Connie, Scott, Carole, Joe, Alicia, and Aurora for their love and support. To those I love who have passed on, but are overseeing my endeavors, T.A. Marlene, Amy, Brent and Sandy, thanks for still being with me.

Last but not least, I thank my Earth family for giving me the lessons that have given me courage, wisdom and strength. Thanks Virg for loving me and keeping your doors open! Without all of your support and faith in me, this book would never have been written.

Virginia's Acknowledgments

I want to thank my wonderful office manager, Alma Scheer, for her commitment in getting this book typed and prepared for publication. She is a stalwart companion and I am forever grateful to have her dedicated talent working with me. I also want to thank our book designer, Ron Cantoni, for his efforts in the production phase, and Gaelyn at Lightbourne for her distinctive book cover and ongoing support. A special acknowledgment goes to my spiritual friends Sam Holland and Anne Claire Venemans for permission to use the grid and ley field/line graphics presented in their book, *Sacred Spaces and Their Universal Connection* available at Altan Publishing, 1614 S.E. 38th Avenue, Portland, OR 97214.

As always, I wish to honor all members of the SHARE Foundation's board of directors, past and present, for their commitment to our networking principles and their support of the publication of nine books through S.E.E. (Spiritual Education Endeavors), our publishing company. I am particularly grateful for the work of our spiritual attorney, John Afton, whose professional clarity and personal caring have been vital to the SHARE Foundation over many years.

For her work on this current book I want to honor my spiritual sister, Orpheus, for completing a project that was intensely challenging. She kept to her intentions through thick and thin, fulfilling a promise made to Archangel Michael long ago. I'm so pleased we were able to finish this important task, dear sister. Profuse congratulations to you!

It is also important for me to acknowledge all of the co-authors of our previous books who have made a valuable contribution to humanity with their own time and energy. You have my unending gratitude for your commitment to our mutual service.

We have been deeply touched over the years to receive donations toward our networking and publishing endeavors. The "thank you's" for their help on this current book go to Immanuel Rainbowlight, the Thorek family, and Donald Stevens. We are genuinely grateful!

Finally, I want to thank all of the metaphysical organizations, writers, speakers, teachers, healers, artists, musicians, scientists, environmentalists, statesmen and other helpers—visible and invisible—who have brought their own wisdom and love to planet Earth. The gifts of these helpmates have enriched my life and aided me in broadening my comprehension of the cosmic nature of existence. Most especially I'm grateful for our magnificent children whose wisdom, innocent love, and joyful light help us remember who we truly are and why we're here for this Earth adventure.

Introducing Orpheus Phylos

Written by Vera Lauren
with respect and deepest devotion!

The Archangel Michael has been with Orpheus Phylos since birth, but it was not until 1980 that he appeared to his oracle, the former Dollye Powers. It has taken a lifetime for their relationship to develop and to prepare her to carry forth his message at this present time. It is difficult for any of us to fathom the significance of this Archangel's effect on her life as a total mentor. One can only imagine the experience, the totality of the absolute trust, and the incredible learning and importance of this student/mentor relationship.

Whether as a frightened child in a dark closet hiding from an abusive father, during out-of-body adventures, recovering from near-death experiences or battling cancer, the Archangel Michael was ever present, protecting and watching over her. The courage and strength she has developed during this journey has taught her the significance of connecting to the oneness of everything, realizing the uselessness of judgment, and the inner knowing that everything is in Divine Right Order.

Her journey began in 1965, when she was twenty-five years old. Frail, weak and weighing only 72 pounds, Dollye was in a hospital hooked up to feeding tubes, dying from anorexia. It was at this low point in her life that she was first awakened by a telepathic voice that said, "You are not dying yet." As this voice spoke there was a cobalt blue sphere about the size of a tennis ball, suspended in the air, about three feet from her face. She felt an indescribable love surround her and she gained a new perspective and inner strength, literally lighting the fire within. This experience gave her the courage to follow her intuition and the permission to severe the bonds that were holding her back.

By 1969, she was developing an interest in astrology, which was her only connection to metaphysics at that time. One Sunday afternoon, she sat alone reading a book when she felt an urge to look up. Three feet away, a cobalt blue sphere about the size of a beach ball was suspended in midair! It was pulsating and emanating rays of light for several minutes before disappearing. This time there was no telepathic message. However, immediately afterwards, Dollye began seeing clusters of sparkling, blinking, blue lights everywhere she went, day or night. The sparkling blue lights came so often that she knew they were signs from spirit that everything would be okay.

Then in May of 1979, Dollye got up during the night feeling disoriented and confused. Her mother and daughter helped her to lie down on the couch and the next thing she knew she was out of her body in a circular room surrounded by many beings. These transparent beings, with large luminous blue eyes, seemed as if they could see right through her, as though they were all-knowing. They were very comforting and reassuring while working on her, as she sat in a translucent crystalline chair.

She was still very much aware of her physical body lying below her on the couch. As she watched from above, she felt electrical currents and saw her physical body being raised a foot off the couch and gently placed back down. On the third lift, they said, "You must go back into your body now." She could feel her spirit slipping back into the body as she telepathically heard a voice say, "You are now prepared." That year was filled with many sleepless nights, the continuous feeling of being out of sync, and a profound awareness that a presence was with her.

A year later, May 22, 1980, in the middle of the night, her entire room lit up, and a robe-like form of energy emanating gold, blue, violet and white light appeared at the side of her bed. Telepathically she heard the comment: "Why are you struggling? We agreed eons ago to come together to do the Father's work." Deep inside her heart and in every cell of her body she recognized this as truth and felt intoxicated by a profoundly intense love. When the light form moved to the foot of the bed, she mentally asked this loving energy, "Can I please see you?" Immediately he appeared, and Dollye recognized him as what she believed to be the face of Christ. This majestic being, with amazing blue eyes, started toward her projecting awesome blue energy rays into her, throwing her into a deep, deep, sleep.

When she woke up the next day the voice in her head said, "Your conceptual thought forms are now ready and prepared." Remember that this experience occurred in the early 1980's when channeling was a "new" phenomenon and it felt really odd to Dollye who had never heard a voice in her head before. Dazed, she went to her mother in the living room and asked her to get a pad and pen, saying, "I don't know what, if anything, is going to happen, but this voice is telling me to sit. I'm just going to sit here and listen to the voice, but be prepared to write if something does occur."

All Dollye remembers was seeing pulsating blue lights and hearing the voice say, "I come." Two hours later she "came to," and her Mother handed her twenty pages of notes she had written. Within those twenty pages the voice announced himself as the one known to man as the Archangel Michael and he outlined five basic steps Dollye was instructed to follow. She was also told she would be meeting people to help her develop, which is exactly what happened in the next week. This mentoring went on for about a year and soon afterward Dollye expanded into lecturing and teaching.

In 1982, Archangel Michael began teaching Dollye to hear telepathically. He also said she would be taking a trip to Arizona from California. In fact, she ended up moving to Arizona but began traveling and teaching in many places.

In 1984, in Crestone, Colorado, Dollye was taking care of a friend's place. That morning she wasn't feeling well and was telepathically instructed to lie down on the couch. She went out-of-body to the "other side" where the Archangel Michael was standing and he asked her to wait. She remembers watching other souls pass by, going to the greater light. Although encircled in great love she was feeling remorse because she did not have time to say goodbye to her two children. When Michael reappeared he told her she would have to return to Earth, because it was not her time yet.

Meanwhile, on Earth, a stranger who was passing by her house smelled gas. He looked in the window, saw Dollye lying motionless, came in and pulled her out. She had stopped breathing. Dollye opened her eyes and watched this stranger breathe but he was not administering CPR. His spiral breathing technique continued awhile and then he stopped and said, "You know you were gone."

He helped her to her feet as friends she had been expecting arrived, and then the stranger left. No one knew him. Later that night Dollye went into trance so friends could ask Michael why this had happened. He explained that Dollye had experienced a soul exchange and she was now Orpheus Phylos! Orpheus means oracular, or oracle—one who communicates, and Phylos, means brotherhood for the new millennium.

Immediately after this experience Orpheus had more stamina and strength for Michael to speak through her for a longer duration. She began traveling all over the world lecturing and taking groups to many of Earth's portals and major vortices located in Greece, Australia, Mexico, Hawaii, Jamaica, South Africa, New Zealand, England, Turkey and Egypt.

Then the unthinkable happened. In October of 1990, Orpheus was diagnosed with cancer and given three months to two years to live. Just before the cancer, she had a dream that she was walking with Michael and he showed her a golden archway. He said, "This is my tabernacle of learning; look above to the words 'know thyself.' I will be taking you into the Christ church to be schooled and you'll be there for a time."

Michael guided her throughout the cancer experience and suggested she use color therapy, music and imagery.

It took several years to recuperate from the trauma of cancer. During those years, Orpheus did some teaching and much inner work. Michael taught her to go within to travel to other worlds, and to see pictures inwardly. Orpheus is more than a voice channel. She telepathically sees visualizations. In this book many of the graphics were conceived this way. Her energies are actually "blended" with those of the Archangel Michael who told her she would be channeling a book. This is that book.

The Archangel Michael channeled this book through Orpheus to bring his message to mankind and to let us know there will be a new world peace through ascension. Most important, he is announcing that he is coming with his Legion of Light to transmute negativity by continuing to neutralize darkness. Man must comprehend that there are many celestial beings and interlaced dimensions working for this great ascension. Divine light will overcome darkness as humanity returns back to God.

With gratitude and humility, Orpheus Phylos honors and values her partnership with God through the Archangel Michael. She continues to carry on the work through spiritual writings, and cosmic teachings.

Virginia's Introduction

As humans living on our exquisite planet, we sometimes become so involved in our personal lives that we forget what an extraordinary creation Earth really is! That is one of the reasons Archangel Michael has chosen to emphasize Earth's values to us in this book. Enclosed in the concrete of our gargantuan cities we may forget she provides everything we need for life. Consider the magnificent green trees and wondrous blue skies that give us breath, the variety of food that springs from her soil, the indispensable waters that quench our thirst, and her awesome scenery that soothes our minds and refreshes our hearts. She is our mother, our home, and we are intimately connected to her, dependent upon her for our very lives.

Yet even as we view her wonders with our eyes and hear her sounds with our ears, Earth's most amazing secrets are hidden from us because we lack the ability to see her energy fields clairvoyantly or hear her voice clairaudiently. It is these hidden secrets, these mysteries she holds, that will be of enormous assistance to our lives in the 21st Century if only we can learn what they are. It is for this very reason that our beloved protector, Archangel Michael, comes forth at this hour to share information about these mysteries with us.

Not only does Earth contain answers and support for our basic personal needs and safety, but she offers an evolutionary vehicle on which we may expand our love and perceptions. Just as a mother is mysterious but essential to the baby within her womb, so Earth is the womb within which our embryonic species moves into a greater expression of higher consciousness—a vibratory frequency necessary in the Cosmos from which she came. Although we are beginning to learn a speck of information about that Cosmos and Earth's relationship to it, both contain inscrutable qualities and unfathomable intentions presently beyond our ken. Thankfully,

Archangel Michael clarifies Earth's true essence, her physical nature and spiritual composition, and that of our own subtle energy bodies in relationship to hers, so we may move more wisely toward that long-promised destiny of peace, compassion and love.

We are beginning to remember more consciously that we are an integral part of Earth and her cosmic lineage, and discovering that we also have our own cosmic genealogy, not just physical heredity and family bloodlines on Earth. It is time to accept both Earth's and our cosmic roots, our family connections in the distant stars, galaxies and inter-dimensions, as a reality. It is the moment to live our lives according to the infinite design we represent in matter.

One day when our eyes can actually see pulsations of living energy—its particles, waves, fields, grids, ley lines, power points, vortices and energy portals—we will finally perceive the composition of our planet's unseen structure. At that instant of relating the wonder of our own subtle body energy fields to Earth's, we will attain a resplendent, universal view of reality and penetrate deeper into the creative qualities of our own species to full advantage.

To aid humanity's clarity about who we really are and why we are here on Earth at this historic hour, Archangel Michael will share helpful information about the energetic realities of Earth and describe the prior civilizations who lived here that have direct bearing on our own existence today. By learning how our own physical and subtle energy fields relate to the Earth's multiple energies and realities, we can integrate our energies with hers for greater physical, emotional, mental and spiritual growth. Indeed, when large numbers of us learn what the Earth's unseen grids, ley lines, vortices, power places, energy points and inter-dimensional portals mean to us, enormous shifts in human consciousness can happen very rapidly...and none too soon!

Our protector will clarify that your soul knew exactly which invisible energies were active in certain locations on

Earth before it descended into physical birth. It knew precisely where the most valuable vibratory influences of color, sound, and other sustaining frequencies would be available on the planet for its life purposes. Can you accept it literally had a map of such energies and could choose, with spiritual guidance, the most conducive area possible for its physical experience? Would such a map be useful to the physical people now embodied here who wanted to remember the reason for their choices? It is hoped that the material Archangel Michael has provided in this book, describing the influential vortex energies in your state of birth—or in locations available in different regions you've experienced since birth—may prove thought provoking, even validating.

How would you feel today if you realized that your place of birth really held palpable energies of color, sound, and valuable spiritual influences? What if you learned that there were powerful vortex entrances in all mountains and elevated sites everywhere on Earth, not just at a few sacred locations? Sites that broadcast frequencies connecting you to both Earth's physical and spiritual influences? In reading this material, perhaps you will grasp the significance of your chosen physical birth location, and your family members there, as part of a pre-planned journey to Earth based on specific soul aspirations.

By exploring such ideas and consciously taking advantage of these energies, would you appreciate your physical existence in more meaningful ways? Have a greater sense of empowerment in living your daily life? If you realized that your present location had both physical and subtle energies affecting you—and you now understood what those energies were for—could you evaluate whether the intended soul influences had been recognized and completed? Would you grasp that your personal choices are not merely based on where a job is located or where your family resides? And would you have the fortitude to affirm your inner knowing by making a decision to move elsewhere if guided to do so?

Never before have so many been called to find their supportive friends, their communities of light! Not only are the subtle and physical influences of an area important, but those awakening compatriots who are your true spiritual comrades from eons past may be found there. These are people like yourself whose soul purposes match your own dedication to life and to the practice of wisdom and love. The composition of such spiritual groups is not based on the similarity of culture, race, religion or gender but on their finest inner qualities desiring expression. It is in finding and sharing with one another that group consciousness that we will coalesce to manifest a broader reality. We now have the choice to be part of a stupendous plan in which the Cosmos and Earth offer us a shift to higher awareness.

If this is true, why aren't more of us listening to our inner guidance that calls us to change, to acquire new perceptions, and move in new directions? Contact with our inner guidance takes time and quietude, two ingredients that most people say are missing in their daily lives. Many of us are so busy that we don't take time to pause in the silence of contemplation or meditation that is essential for opening to our great inner knowledge.

Sometimes we have a vague feeling that we need to be elsewhere doing something different, but we don't stop to experience that feeling at any serious depth. Or we may simply ignore our inner yearnings because we believe that we must stay on our present job, retain our current commitments. Perhaps we are tied to payments for a home, car, and any number of other material possessions. We may say we are trapped in a stressful life, yet lack the courage or wisdom to modify it. We may feel helpless in the intensity of our self-created circumstances, failing to realize we can decide to change them. Some of us are even acquiring health problems that will become chronic, even deadly, yet we ignore the signals to alter our lifestyle until pain and suffering require it.

Without the willingness to transform some aspects of existence, the days and hours rush by without serious contemplation of what our soul is attempting to communicate, and we don't take advantage of that soulful information that would give us a sense of guidance and certainty. In any direction we look, our species is being challenged to utilize the immense creative power of our nature with discipline and fervor—and to escape the entrapment of our materialistic societies. It is the momentous hour, now, for us to explore our character, our vision, and our commitment to human evolution. Yes, and to somehow maximize the extraordinary upgrade in consciousness that is being offered to those of us on Earth.

It is a profound and opportune moment in human history that calls our individual name and requests the resurgence of group cooperation, respect, and compassion. More than ever we are offered the scenario in which to practice the age-old commandment to love God and one another! Regardless of where you are in the continuum of growth, we hope that the information and energy contained in this book will add support to your personal desire to claim your innate love and creativity and to take your place on the platform of service to life. We also hope to inspire those people standing on the brink of genuine self-discovery to trust their first step forward in these exciting times of transformation.

In the contents of this book we hope to have you confirm that:

• You are part of an embryonic species advancing into higher consciousness.

• You are more than a physical body—you have both consciousness and various subtle energy fields that allow a simultaneous physical, emotional and spiritual existence.

• You have energy in your physical body as well as subtle (less dense) energy fields around your body, but you are greater than both your physical and subtle body fields, and the chakras that connect them.

• You are a celestial being, a soul who has an enormous "lifestream" of experience attained through physical embodiment on Earth or other planets, or dimensions beyond Earth.

• Your greater spiritual essence knows you can have contact with spiritual beings existing in what might be termed the "Inner Worlds" of our planet.

• Your true identity also has the capacity to contact non-physical beings of high consciousness in innumerable spiritual dimensions of reality connected to Earth herself and also to the Cosmos beyond.

Later in this document Archangel Michael will define such terms as star children, star lights, and star seeds and will explain how Earth's physical and spiritual qualities are an essential part of your cosmic roots, your daily life. It is absolutely necessary to grasp the way she functions and to utilize Earth's grids, ley lines, vortices, sacred sites, entry portals, doorway frequencies, and even mountain influences and energies that impact upon various local and global regions.

This is fascinating and useful information for everyone regardless of where they live on the planet. It is especially appropriate right now when we need to grasp just how profoundly our planet's vortices and mountain energies affect human consciousness, how they can help us unveil our innate spiritual abilities, and how they can provide safety zones. As we will learn, there are forces at work from the very throne of God to assist many galaxies and their species during this time of uplifting consciousness and energy resources.

Archangel Michael will also include compelling information about 9 planetary systems beyond Earth including Maldek. He will also clarify the value of our historical and spiritual experiences in the formative era of Lemuria. Descriptions of the famous healing temples of Lemuria are included to help bring back valuable healing practices needed today. Since the early Lemurian energies and consciousness birthed many other civilizations whose influences are with us still, there will be clarification about the Atlantean and pre-dynasty Egyptian influences and their current effects now. Although some of those earlier cultural influences are very positive, others are quite the opposite and still affect the consciousness level of many humans. The rigidity of old hatreds, fears, violence, materialism, and control over others remains today, even in the midst of an increasingly positive attitude for a peaceful global citizenry. The challenge is to remain balanced and complete the purposes we came to model.

* * *

While none of us in human form can fully perfect the messages we bring from celestial dimensions, Orpheus and I are combining our efforts to empower the highest possible energy resonance receptivity with Archangel Michael. Orpheus has been his channel for nearly 20 years and we have been together on various occasions during that period. In 1989, I published Archangel Michael's taped messages as a chapter in the book <u>New Cells, New Bodies, New Life!</u> Now Orpheus brings his book length revelations for the new millennium.

My own role in the following chapters is to integrate Archangel Michael's material from Orpheus, assemble it into readable form, and ask some questions without changing the meaning or losing the vibratory effect. Orpheus and I hope our partnership in this venture will bring you value. May your soul's love and inspiration expand your own gifts to life and continue to guide and protect you throughout eternity.

Contents

| Chapter 1 | The Archangel Michael Speaks .... 1 |

Chapter 2   Mirror of Venus and the Four Corners 21

Chapter 3   The Overshadowing City 37

Chapter 4   Your Life on Earth with the
Harmonic Grids 55

Chapter 5   The Tribunal Godhead and the
Holographic Computer 71

Chapter 6   The Planetary Systems and Maldek 85

Chapter 7   Lemuria 107

Chapter 8   Migration to Atlantis and Egypt 127

Chapter 9   The Seven Worlds of Graduation 141

Chapter 10   Coming Times 157

Chapter 11   Ascension and the Spiral of Infinity 177

> If you knew that there was an adventure to help you remember your inherent wholeness and life-giving spiritual essence, would you be willing to start exploring it?

Chapter 1

The Archangel Michael Speaks

I am the one you call Archangel Michael, the protector, who sits on the right hand of the Universal Father/Mother. I have been appointed by the Great One to bring forth the universal law of free will and free choice, just as Lucifer stands on the left side to create opposition, so that the spiral of infinity or everlasting life can continue forward.

I come from the Central Sun beyond your Universe, or as you understand it, from the seat of God, using the power of breath that extends beyond time into timelessness. My breath of energy is of the size of a galaxy permeating through many dimensions, planes and angelic realms. For this reason I am called Christ Michael of your Universe. I have been appointed to keep the spiral of everlasting life active by continuing to neutralize darkness, transmute negativity, oversee the Universe, and create new worlds. I hold the power of the Sun, which is known to you on Earth as the element of fire/ nitrogen. This fire comes from the higher heaven and is known in your present scientific understanding as proton, neutron and electron. This power of the Great One has been called Father, Son and Holy Ghost or Spirit—manifesting itself on Earth through the element of fire/nitrogen.

1

When you look deep inside the flame of a candle, you will see the golden radiance of the flame glowing, just as you see the gold of your sun shining up in the sky. But if you look deeper within the flame's center you will also see a blue hue which symbolizes the radiating deep indigo blue of the actual Central Sun that is millions of light years away from your Earth. In ways difficult for you to perceive, I am the holder of the transmutable blue flame, the flame of the Central Source, which some of you call God. This blue flame is now interpenetrating the Earth plane in preparation for my coming to uplift the souls of humanity, to connect them to their spiritual reality, and to teach them how to release the chains of bondage and darkness.

I want you to know that you are not separated from God as some would have you believe, but that you are one with the "greatness of breath" that resides within you. It is this breath that you breathe that is the everlasting life force pulsation that allows you, as soul, to come and experience, experiment and be the very expression of God through your physical embodiments. As you let go of the outside world and find the path that takes you to the kingdom within, you will then begin to walk with the preciousness of light, the flower of life, which is the consciousness of oneness or God.

As you are surrounded in this light you no longer hold prejudices, judgment or even self-judgment, but will only emanate pure love. There are those of you upon the Earth plane who can, and will, awaken to be the illuminators, to carry the sword of truth and demonstrate the beingness of love. Amazingly, by utilizing the gifts of spirit to serve humankind, you will create a greater world of peace and harmony called the New Age, Golden Dawn, or Millennium of Peace. This new world era will be a time when the consciousness of God will reign supreme and there will no longer be duality and negativity, but a one world consciousness of divine wisdom and peace.

Then I come to gather all the illuminaries, the Christ souls, who are the saints of the latter days. You are the ones who will awaken into your Christ selves, and walk the path of eternal light only worshiping the supreme Creator of all things. You will no longer allow the opposition of duality to distract, deter, or to discourage you, but will see the falsity of the disguises of lower nature negativity and will overcome fear that binds you to the dimension of Earth. Another world soon comes, and love is the only key that will open the gates to this higher kingdom.

The veil of your heavens will be torn open, and as far as humanity can see, you will see the lords, angelic hosts within hosts, Holies of Holies, Elohim, Yahweh, and the presence of pure love and light. So be ready and continue to love your heavenly Father/Mother, your soul and the precious breath that is ever present within you. NO ONE KNOWS the exact moment when we will physically come until the Creator's word is spoken—not even I, the Archangel Michael—but its word will be heard by all of heaven. Be assured that when that great signal comes I will call upon all of my Legions of Light throughout the whole of the Universe and the confrontation between darkness and light will be at hand.

Know that I will come and uplift the souls who have stood strong and united for peace, positive free will, and love—regardless of race, gender, creed or religion. I will come for them because as awakened souls they recognized that the eternal light shines within every living soul and that expressing love is the key of light that opens the doors of a new kingdom. Many religions, epics and myths relate to this possibility of my coming, in their different ways, and each account contains an underlying cord of truth to keep hope alive for a longing humanity.

In your biblical information you are told that God created the heavens and the Earth and made two great lights: the greater light to rule the day and the lesser light to rule the night. I, Archangel Michael, am the Prince of Peace of the heavenly kingdom and Lucifer is the Prince of Earth, prince of the lower worlds. You are also told that God made the stars and set them into the firmament of heaven to give light upon the Earth to rule over the day and over the night. Then, as the light was divided from the darkness this created duality and separation. This means that the Earth is an emotional plane where souls can use free will to experience the opposite of light and then choose to return home through the tests of time.

This separation of light and dark began the interplay of free will and free choice so the spiral of life on Earth could be activated and the Creator could see itself expressed throughout all planes of life, even the dense matter worlds.

Because Earth began as a three-dimensional frequency, the Creator used three aspects to make up the human body—the physical, mental and emotional. Through this "body of clay"—or carbon-based vessel—a soul could enter to experience emotion, or energy-in-motion, and live in the world of feeling for the first time. Since the celestial kingdoms do not experience physical sensation, touch or physical feelings, entering this lower vibratory world would be an enormous and challenging adventure for the souls who chose the density of Earth. Since the Father/Mother holds the Earth plane in great reverence, souls who have come into this emotional experience, and still expressed their sacredness of love, will grow 10 million fold.

Souls who chose the Earth plane for a specified incarnation cycle of about 250,000 years knew that they would be entering a school to test their mastery of transmuting negativity into light—or using cosmic mind over matter—even in the third dimension. To support their incarnation on Earth these souls placed all prior knowledge about their creation, and other life experiences, into a "fail-safe" system so they would *not* remember blissful memories of their great spiritual qualities and attributes while embarked into a free choice density. As spiritual beings on Earth, these humans would have to use their higher mind over negative emotions to be able to ascend to higher worlds before the end of the 250,000 year divine cycle.

Now, as this great cycle of incarnation begins to close for

everyone on Earth, many are being drawn to spiritual teachings of all kinds in many different forms—meditations, books, movies, lectures and so on. You are feeling the soul's urging to awaken and are making more frequent connections to inner guidance, to your teachers, guides, gurus, angels and the energy of God's love itself. Since the Earth's vibrations are heightening and many humans are remembering the Creator's plan, we are coming to give you inspiration and to support your healing needs and intuitive developments. Please understand that this cyclical, divine intervention allows a greater protection and assistance than humans have had for eons. Enjoy it! And know that the peers of heaven are committed to humanity's graduation.

As your protector, one of the most helpful things I can do for humanity at this time, through my oracle, Orpheus, is to share the love of the Great One, and ask you to hold fast to your own divinity. But I also come to explain the structure of the Earth's energy fields which have been profoundly affecting you every day of your life—and which you greatly need to use during this transformational time. Most of all, I invite you to appreciate your enormously beautiful Earth sphere and her many historical and spiritual mysteries.

I ask you to perceive that she has many vital relationships in the brotherhood of cosmic life and to value her as a sentient, purposeful being with qualities and characteristics you need to use more consciously. And most expressly I want you to know she is filled with, and surrounded by, spiritual beings who actually assist her—and your own—ascension. Too often humans presume that they are ascending directly into heavenly regions without recognizing and utilizing the enormous support that exists in your Earth's spiritual realms. Indeed, many of you will use Earth's energy portals of light in order to leave the lower dimensional worlds behind. For this reason I will now specifically devote attention to the physical and sacred qualities of your superlative homeland.

Let me begin by asking you to imagine your extraordinary planet from afar, as your astronauts have done from space, and see her spherical physical shape with colors of blue, green, brown and white—turning like a jewel in space. This image is now familiar to most humans yet Earth has a deeper identity that I wish to share with the general population regarding her grids.

As you look at the following black and white illustration of Earth's form covered in energy grids please imagine those grid lines to be shining in the brightest multi-colored radiance imaginable with the colors emanating a melodious symphony. As you imagine this, you might well be wondering where this glorious grid comes from and how it affects humans and other life forms. **(See Illustration #1)**

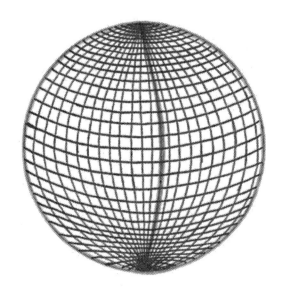

Illustration #1 - Planet Earth with Grid Lines

At the time of Earth's creation (first called Shawn) the grids that encircle her were placed there because she had to be energized and interconnected with the Cosmos. The Ya-na-nee-nees, who were the first group of higher vibratory beings ever to dwell on Earth, had to activate these grids to allow their entrance and exit process to other celestial systems. Later on, after the Logos and Adamic civilizations, physical-etheric beings called Lemurians, were Earth's first long-term residents and I will include an entire chapter about the Lemurians later on in my message. For now I simply want to clarify that when these high vibratory beings came into the density of Earth, they had to rearrange the Earth's frequency to maintain their telepathic modes of communication and their orbital grid patterns. Therefore, crystals were inlaid throughout the Earth to create the grid, ley field, ley line systems they needed for entering and exiting the Earth plane and for providing a system to maintain the planet's orbital stability. Over time Earth changes have caused damage and disturbances to these grids which we are strengthening even as I speak.

As a result of the 1994 comet impact on Jupiter many of the Earth's vortices that were not active are now being awakened or activated. For example, the North Pole has been active for a long time and has been used as one of the main pathways for entering and exiting your planet. Now the South Pole will be activated so you will see more activity by your angelic friends. Activating the grid systems will assist many upon Earth to receive clearer telepathic thoughts from her inner spiritual dimensions thus giving you the ability to awaken to your greater gifts of sensitivity, telepathic communication, radionics, higher technology and healing.

Understand that the Earth plane is now being lifted into a higher vibratory acceleration which means that Earth's solidity (carbon) is now being rearranged so that matter can be changed into silicon (crystal light). Therefore, planet Earth is graduating, and once again joining the higher heavens. As a consequence, all the souls who let go of negativity can become one in divine love and also arise in Earth's great ascension.

Because the electro-magnetic fields throughout the Universe will now be enhanced to a higher vibration, the effect will quicken Earth's grid activity to a higher vibration—and will also magnify the ley lines of your planet to a higher frequency. **(See Illustration #2)**

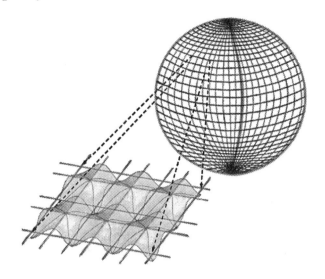

Illustration #2 - Earth's Grids with Ley Fields

Therefore, all megalithic and monolithic structures, pyramids, kivas, ancient ruins, and many of the great sacred mountains are now being energized to a higher vibration. These are what we call major "lots" or sites that hold a grid of powerful energy that can be utilized for many purposes. As humans look upon these ancient sites many think of them simply as a physically solid wonderment, but many of these sites, or vortices, hold hidden doorways into the Inner World dimensions of Earth. Some of these vortices you would recognize in America are the Rocky Mountains, the Tetons, the Santa Christos Mountains and Mount Shasta, but worldwide there are many more.

These grids hold ley fields (composed of ley lines) of energy that connect to each other through a kind of spider web formation thus connecting the major sites or vortices that vibrate frequencies into the power points.

These power points being carried within the electro-magnetic fields are geographically connected to major vortex sites. These points connect at every 15 degrees longitude and latitude on your globe. Each power point has a parallel to a higher frequency or an area of greater size at division points of 30, 60, 90, 120, and 180 degrees. At the 180 degree point where the longitude and latitude points intersect, this encompasses all four quadrants of the energy grids throughout the world, and the ley lines work in unison creating a major vortex of energy. Major vortex sites are the strength of the grid formation. Still the spider web formation, as a working unit, is an incredible thought communicator as the many ley lines disperse units of coded frequencies.

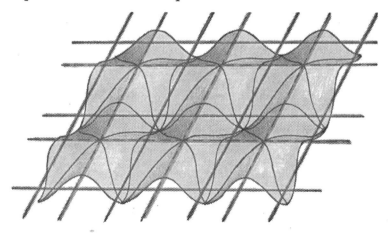

Illustration #3 - Ley Fields

As you look at the illustration of a ley field, composed of ley lines, **(See Illustration #3)** please notice that it is capable of warping or movement. This affects humanity. Specific ley fields divide a grid square into 4 parts or quadrants. You can think of each of these 4 quadrants as being an element of earth, fire, water or air. When the end points of earth and water form 2 poles and the air and fire form 2 poles, these 4 elemental quadrants form a 4-pole magnet. This is critical to the Earth because if she needs a release from stress and pressure, the ley fields warp—bend, twist, curve or turn—thereby creating a tension that causes a physical reaction to relieve it. I want you to appreciate that the Creator has designed a motif of cooperation and interaction between the electrical and magnetic properties of Earth's grid and ley lines. This assures that when electrical or magnetic tensions occur during Earth's movement through space, or when her inhabitants are destructive in thought and deed, this carefully designed planet can release her negative stress by means of familiar human experiences such as storms, floods, volcanoes and earthquakes.

Although none of you may want to be at the effect of Earth's various reactions to stress, kindly remember they are beneficial for both humanity and Earth as you move within the cosmic rhythms and cycles that interconnect life throughout the solar system, galaxy and beyond. In this network of the evolving divine plan, never underestimate your nurturing role as a dominion-keeper of Earth and all other life. What you think and how you behave in loving ways are not only important aspects of your own personal mastery, but they also influence your planet and the tapestry of life beyond time and space. *While many of you realize that you hold a deepening relationship with heaven, it is now vital to comprehend what Earth's unseen physical and spiritual energies offer you, and to utilize them wisely. Earth is both your physical womb and your matrix to her invisible spiritual cities and Inner Worlds.* This current cycle is a powerful time to remember and embrace her many secret doorways and portals to dimensions unseen!

When you visit particular pyramids, sacred sites and mountains, you are utilizing physical points on the Earth's invisible grid that connect you to powerful vortex energies. But there are also other unseen vortices or portals and spiritual doorways everywhere present on Earth, not just those marked with physical structures. These generally have energy flows within defined parameters of influence. These spiraling energy flows exist everywhere and can range from very small to quite huge in their influence and purpose. You have developed small ones in your own meditation or personal prayer space, and even larger vortices where groups of loving people meet. Yet without your knowledge or control, huge vortices are automatically flowing in all mountains, hills, and elevated locations around the planet, even in the deserts and oceans. **(See Illustration #4 on the next page)** In this illustration you can see a few of the pyramids and important sacred site vortices that humans often visit. Have you been especially drawn to any of these places?

Of course many more mountains and pyramids were located on the grid system that once existed when Earth was a single land mass. Occasionally your scientists can locate these physical buildings under water. There have been massive destructions by prior civilizations that thrust vast land portions of the Earth, and the pyramids, into the oceans and seas. Because it is so difficult for humanity to enter the depths of these waters to see what they look like, you must rely upon technical instruments to report their existence or believe inspirational messages brought by channeled sources. Even so, there are many pyramid and sacred sites still located upon every remaining continent that await discovery. Many are hidden in jungles covered with vegetation; others have been disguised by the changes in mountain areas and soil redistribution. In China alone great numbers of pyramids still remain to be explored.

In the last few years many awakening humans are deliberately traveling to major vortices and sacred sites, or to holy places contained in particular churches and temples. Some of these amplified energy spots have been identified by earlier cultures and built upon to indicate recognition of their value. Or their powerful energy can simply draw certain people to them as a soul recognition event—a remembrance of profound import. Many are located in the world's great mountains, of course, but even smaller hills and deserts have vortices whose energies assist in strengthening Earth and its inhabitants.

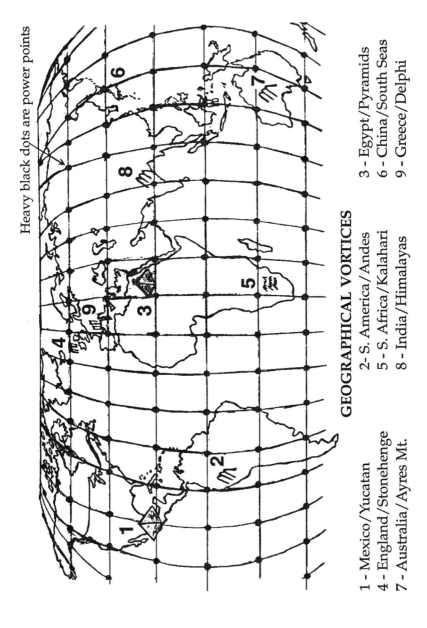

Illustration #4 - Geographical Vortices of Sacred Sites

While the height of the mountain or mountain range generally indicates its intensity and power, there are exceptions. Because these vortices can affect a local or regional area, even a state or a nation, we will list the vortices just within the U.S. borders as an example of how they affect you wherever you choose to live. **(See Table #1, next two pages)** If you are not living in the United States please look at a local map of your own country and appreciate what your mountain vortex areas give you in energy.

I hope you are beginning to understand that Earth and humanity are inexorably connected. You each affect the other. The vortices aid the development of your inner spiritual quest and the extension of your God-given consciousness. In addition, you are both related to other consciousness and places far beyond Earth's borders. You are truly related to many sentient beings throughout creation by the level of your own vibratory frequency.

I have now briefly described some information about grids, ley lines, and vortices which I ask you to contemplate. Even if you do not understand it all—or find it confusing—I ask you to remember one thing. They are vital to both Earth's balance and advancement and to your own health and soulful awareness. You and she are inexorably connected to each other because her many-leveled energies support your body and your very soul during its visit into the density of matter. There are energies around and inside Earth that are your helpmates to higher states of consciousness!

Earth holds many mysteries you are just beginning to discover and I will discuss some of them in the next chapter. One of them is called the Mirror of Venus. This area is related to a part of the western United States that has particularly powerful energies for supporting the establishment of new centers of light in the fields of health, education and technology. I shall share more about the Four Corners area and the Mirror of Venus in the following chapter.

STATE	Color Vibration	High Point	Elevation (Feet above Sea Level)
ALABAMA	green	Cheaha Mt.	2,407
ALASKA	pastels	Mt. McKinley	20,320
ARIZONA	yellow	Humphreys Pk.	12,633
ARKANSAS	yellow	Magazine Mt.	2,753
CALIFORNIA	violet	Mt. Whitney	14,491
COLORADO	orange	Mt. Elbert	14,433
CONNECTICUT	red	Mt. Frissell	2,380
DELAWARE	indigo	New Castle Co. *	442
FLORIDA	silver	Walton Co. *	345
GEORGIA	burgundy	Brasstown Bald	4,784
HAWAII	indigo	Mauna Kea	13,796
IDAHO	red	Borah Peak	12,662
ILLINOIS	pastels	Charles Mound	1,235
INDIANA	violet	Wayne Co. *	1,257
IOWA	yellow	Osceola Co. *	1,670
KANSAS	silver	Mt. Sunflower	4,039
KENTUCKY	silver	Black Mt.	4,145
LOUISIANA	silver	Driskill Mt.	535
MAINE	indigo	Mt. Katahdin	5,268
MARYLAND	violet	Backbone Mt.	3,360
MASSACHUSETTS	indigo	Mt. Greylock	3,491
MICHIGAN	red	Mt. Curwood	1,980
MINNESOTA	silver	Eagle Mt.	2,310
MISSISSIPPI	green	Woodall Mt.	806
MISSOURI	indigo	Tam Sauk Mt.	1,772

Table #1 - List of USA Vortices and Color Vibrations
Note: Color vibrations will be discussed in Chapter 4.
* high point is unnamed, but located in the county shown

STATE	Color Vibration	High Point	Elevation (Feet above Sea Level)
MONTANA	indigo	Granite Peak	12,799
NEBRASKA	burgundy	Kimball Co. *	5,426
NEVADA	silver	Boundary Peak	13,143
NEW HAMPSHIRE	green	Mt. Washington	6,288
NEW JERSEY	violet	High Point Mt.	1,803
NEW MEXICO	yellow	Wheeler Peak	13,161
NEW YORK	yellow	Mt. Marcy	5,344
NORTH CAROLINA	green	Mt. Mitchell	6,684
NORTH DAKOTA	red	White Butte	3,506
OHIO	silver	Campbell Hill	1,550
OKLAHOMA	green	Black Mesa	4,973
OREGON	silver	Mt. Hood	11,239
PENNSYLVANIA	burgundy	Mt. Davis	3,213
RHODE ISLAND	red	Jerimoth Hill	812
SOUTH CAROLINA	yellow	Sassafras Mt.	3,560
SOUTH DAKOTA	pastels	Harney Peak	7,242
TENNESSEE	violet	Clingmans Dome	6,643
TEXAS	indigo	Guadalupe Peak	8,751
UTAH	pwdr blue	Kings Peak	13,528
VERMONT	burgundy	Mt. Mansfield	4,393
VIRGINIA	burgundy	Mt. Rogers	5,729
WASHINGTON	green	Mt. Rainer	14,410
WEST VIRGINIA	yellow	Spruce Knob	4,863
WISCONSIN	burgundy	Timms Hill	1,952
WYOMING	violet	Gannett Peak	13,804

Table #1 continued - List of USA Vortices and Color Vibrations
* high point is unnamed, but located in the county shown

But first, Virginia, are there questions you would like to ask on what has been given?

* * *

Virginia: (hereafter, **VE**) Greetings to you, beloved protector, Archangel Michael, and thank you for this stimulating information. And yes, I do have some questions. First of all, for Christians who believe Christ Jesus is their personal savior and the son of God, does what you say about yourself as being Christ of the Universe demote him to a lesser importance?

Archangel Michael: (hereafter, **AM**) No. It is only humanity that has stations of separation. Where I am, we are in Oneness, and there is no separation. Each of us holds the flame of God, created with specific positions to personify and express that Oneness. I am an eternal who will never take a physical form, but will always remain an energy of light personified by the source of the Central Sun. Jesus is the son/sun (radiant being) who was chosen to come forth as the living personification of God to bring Earth the demonstration of ultimate love. We are a collective energy interlaced as one in service to the living flame of eternity. Our service, with others of the celestial hierarchy, is assisting in the constant evolution of awakening humans at this time to exhilarate the souls of Earth.

VE: So Christians shouldn't feel that Jesus is less just because you have the power of bringing forth the blue flame of God.

AM: Let me clarify. There are those who are known as the chief princes, kings of righteousness or high chiefs of the Universe. I, Michael, the Chief of Princes, Melchizedek and Jesus of Nazareth are joined together by the Divine. Know that Jesus the Christ is coming for those who will live and demonstrate divinity's true teachings, in order to begin a world of peace in which he will be the executive or overseer. We, the Legions of Light, will all come when the word is spoken.

It is now time for all leaders of religious orders to come

together, to let go of their different convictions and to know they are seeking the same light. This light of Oneness or love is the only key that will open the door of heaven. The teachings of Christ Jesus did not sanction hate, torture, imprisonment, killing, lovelessness, or wars in his name.

VE: When you describe Lucifer as the Prince of Earth and the lower worlds, is that an archetypal or anthropomorphic way of looking at Lucifer? Is Lucifer actually present among us? Or is it just his thought forms working on Earth?

AM: Lucifer goes to and from the Earth stirring the pot of negativity by dropping unloving thought forms, through temptation and disguise, for anyone to utilize and manifest. The greatest tool of Lucifer is what we call the multiple D's of darkness, such as doubt, discouragement, distraction, discomfort, disease, depression, and much more. For example, Jesus was sent out to fast for 40 days and nights in preparation for his greater works, but several days through his journey he heard a voice asking "Why are you suffering so; why do you not eat?" Immediately, Jesus recognized that it was Lucifer and replied "Get behind me. I am about my Father's business." He recognized that a negative thought had come into his mind in order to deter and distract him from his purpose, but he would not allow any disruptive thoughts to discourage him from continuing forward.

All of you are facing your own individual negativity, which comes from the root or base of fear. Lucifer implants negative thoughts into human minds, swaying you out of balance, working on the weak points of personality to create havoc and disruptions in your life. There are many lower nature souls who live on the Earth who have not risen into a consciousness of light, and they are falling into the dark path of evil. Be awake and aware when a negative thought drops into your mind! Do not entertain it. Recognize who and what it is, and then send it on its way while you continue your journey in fulfilling your soul's mission in love.

VE: When we say our prayers or meditate is there a

difference between saying "Father," compared to saying both "Father/Mother?"

AM: Yes. There is a difference in vibration. The patriarch vibration has been upon the Earth for a long time, because of the separation into duality. In duality the masculine became the dominant factor because brute force or physical strength was needed to build and create. In truth, Oneness is both Mother and Father, masculine and feminine. So now the Father/Mother vibration brings the concepts of equality and oneness back together again. Why does the word she have he in it? Why does the word female contain the word male? Simply because the feminine energy is the womb that holds Oneness. It is through the feminine aspect of God's oneness that birthed multiple souls into creation. When you say Father/Mother it is inclusive of both and was Christ Jesus' own salutation to the Creator when he prayed in his native Aramaic language.

VE: Changing the subject, how have the prior pole shifts affected the Earth's grids and vortices? How and why do these pole shifts happen?

AM: Many of these pole shifts occur because of humanity's mistreatment of Earth over which you hold sacred dominion. You cannot experiment with exploding nuclear and atomic devices placed beneath your oceans, or in the atmosphere above, and not expect to create an imbalance of the tectonic plates or ruin the oxygen levels. There are some experiments that disrupt the natural flow of Earth's energy patterns thus creating earthquakes, weather disturbances, despoiling the ozone layers, destroying the rain forests, and so forth. By these deeds humanity can destroy itself.

There is also a natural growth pattern that occurs within the elements of Earth that must rearrange when appropriate. Of course, there are shifts occurring in your stratosphere and throughout the solar system that cause a ripple effect upon Earth. But at this time, humans are causing the majority of disruptive forces ecologically depleting Earth from her natural flow of well-being.

VE: Having said that, are we likely to have a pole shift soon?

AM: I will not give an exact time because it depends on the collective consciousness of humanity as to when this may occur. However, there is a vibration of a global shift to take place that could possibly cause enough upheaval to rearrange the ocean floors and create the rising of old Atlantis. If humanity would change its ways, however, many of the prophetic events could be avoided.

VE: Thank you. Please explain what is required in preparing a person's body, such as Orpheus', to become a good trance channel for higher frequencies and not be harmed in any way. Because many people are trance channeling, I thought it would be useful to explain that process.

AM: Orpheus and I have been together for many eons, in many lifetimes, during which she has been trained to connect with my frequency without too much readjustment. Each embodiment, of course, requires balance, which is learned by letting go and letting God, or by trusting. First the souls create an agreement to be in partnership and to join together at a particular time. They usually connect to deliver philosophy and other appropriate messages from the spiritual worlds. When spirit comes it will assist the vessel in developing its higher aspects, therein sharing the information spirit wishes to deliver. In reality, we are all one, so it just takes fine-tuning to activate the partnership.

Not everyone on Earth is meant to be a telepathic/voice channel because it takes an incredible amount of patience, dedication, and trust to go through the process of uniting. Some want the experience because it seems appealing, but few are serious enough to give up their way of life and become an active vessel for spirit. Spirit is very aware of how to utilize the body and teaches the vessel to proceed cautiously. Individualized suggestions are given on how to take care of the body as they connect and work together. Spirit will work slowly until the comfort level is found that opens to other states of development.

If anyone comes into an uncomfortable experience, it's because they are holding their own improper thought forms and perceptions, or because they are out of balance mentally or emotionally. Many people are simply not ready to open themselves for this kind of activity and will experience some levels of discomfort especially if they are motivated through an over-expressive ego. There are also those whom you call "conscious" channels meaning they telepathically receive impressions and information to be shared with others. These channels are often dedicated to one specific mentor in spirit for the delivery of inspirational or scientific information.

If you are open to your soul or spirit everyone is a channel to some degree, whether as an artist, musician, writer, speaker, inventor, philosopher, scientist or healer, etc. This is because spirit has gifted them with knowledge that is being expressed through their minds and bodies. An actor or actress takes on a temporary personality of the individual they are portraying and becomes another person only while they are playing the role. Trance mediumship is quite different from play acting because the person must give up much of their own ego preferences in order to have two energies residing in one body. But all levels of channeling and inspiration are intended to bring spiritual comfort, hope, and understanding to the human family during their visits into the density of matter.

Now let me share the good news about the Mirror of Venus and the Four Corners area.

> If you recognized that there was a specific location on the planet that could give you greater energy to awaken to higher consciousness, would you go there?

Chapter 2

Mirror of Venus and the Four Corners

Before humankind lived upon the Earth's surface, there had been many star celestials who colonized Earth when it had a far lighter or more subtle energy vibration than Earth has now. At that time the planet was called Shawn. These first celestials who colonized and lived upon Shawn were a race of beings who came from a celestial system called Yananeenee. They were highly evolved beings who enjoyed traversing the universes so they did not remain long on your planet. Eventually they left Shawn and interfaced with the executives of your Universe, for they had the ability to calculate the energy levels of time lags to cause a cessation point within space-time to catapult into timelessness. The Yananeenees worked together as mind energizers traversing the routed ley lines of different fields of energetic passages. Because many of these needed to be reconnected into other force fields of activity this created an oscillation of the ley lines that opened passages of time, and eventually these celestial beings shifted their energy and transcended into another universe.

Later in Earth's colonization those we call the Logos came and colonized the planet Shawn. These were huge giants and are mentioned in your myths. They had only one eye located in the center of their forehead, meaning their third eye was opened, and they could use it to see into the vistas of many worlds. The Logos who dwelled on Shawn were known as the calculus mathematicians, skilled in the rearrangement of matter into a space continuum of timelessness. In working on this process over a long period of time, they eventually rearranged matter into energy, energy into space-time, and space-time into timelessness. This created multiple openings simultaneously and they instantly ascended into another universal system of light. Fortunately some did choose to stay behind and they are still within your Earth's Inner World dominions assisting with the building of "time cities" to aid humanity in the days ahead.

*Time cities are light cities located **inside** the inner dominion of planet Earth where some light workers will reside until the rhythms of an adverse situation pass by and the souls are released to continue their journey or begin their next life experience.* What I am saying is that Earth has many portals and vortices that will open into these beautiful Inner World cities allowing certain people to enter in for safety until the Earth's surface is finished with its purification. This means that for the purpose of protection some light workers will evacuate or disappear from sight in the twinkling of an eye.

Since the Yananeenees and Logos eras, the planet Earth has had many colonies and settlements, most of which you know little or nothing about for two reasons. First, the colonists were physical-etheric beings who left no physical evidence behind in the third dimension. Second, those who were physical and had civilizations with physical buildings often underwent great destruction. Few traces are still visible since the tectonic plate shifts have rearranged Earth's geological structure into unconnected continents. Everything else is under water or covered by the shifting terrain of mountain or soil debris.

Because Earth's earliest colonists were beings whose consciousness was at a very high vibratory rate, with little physical body density, their needs were not as physically oriented as yours are today. To you they would be invisible. Furthermore, they were telepathic and some even used a pictography language that did not require written words and messages, as you presently know them. I hope you can understand this concept because at their levels of frequency there was no *linear time*, only space-time. I am unable to give you exact dates for these early ancestors but to serve your intellectual need, I would suggest it was millions of years ago. These colonists were, by your limited five senses, timeless beings so a specific physical linear time measurement is inadequate.

More recently, an important epoch began when certain Venusians came to the Earth bringing with them a symbol called the Mirror of Venus. This symbol is what you presently call the ankh and it was later taken by the Lemurians to Egypt where it was used to symbolize eternal life. But the Mirror of Venus was far more than just the symbol of eternal life, because it held a secret within its angles and the configuration of its lines that was a message from the Cosmos. Today, when you look at the ankh you will see four L-shaped lines with the third and fourth L lines wrapped back into a circle. **(See Illustration #5)** The circle represents the Cosmos and the omnipresence of being. The L's represent Law, Life, Light, and Love. The symbol of the ankh also represents the masculine polarity and the oval circle represents the feminine, both enmeshed as one, and yet depicting the duality of each formed separately into the world of illusion.

Illustration #5 - The Ankh

The Mirror of Venus was later used by the Lemurians and Atlanteans as a symbol reminding them of their home in the higher worlds and also as their code of divine love and the oneness of eternal life. Therefore, the mirror has a two-sided meaning. One side held the mysteries of the Cosmos and the reality of the spiritual world's divine love. The other side held the power of the illusory matter world into which these celestials would soon be entering. In other words, the ankh held both forces of the polarities. They realized no one would know the ankh's true meaning until the time came to awaken from their deep illusory sleep and begin to unveil their memories of being from another plane of existence, another dimension.

Over many eras of time, different religions and belief systems changed the top portion of the ankh from a circle of oneness to a straight line. This original ankh symbol was discarded and others were designed like the Crux Ansanta, the Qabbalistic Cross, the Cross of the Druids, the Celtic Cross, the Cross of Liberation, and the Christian Cross—all crosses that have been used throughout time in many nations for religious purposes. Furthermore, as a human being stands upright with its arms outstretched it forms the Cross of Mankind as illustrated by Leonardo da Vinci. The outstretched arms of the human body symbolize the horizontal physical world or the lower heaven, which is vertically connected to the higher body of the heavens of creation. It is important to understand that your physical body also holds an invisible grid formation that can be understood through the symmetrical formula of mathematics. Each organ or body part holds different vibrations that interlace together connecting the body to the whole of spirit.

Those early Venusian colonists knew that when they experienced the Earth's realm of duality, the ankh would be an encoded key to the greater mysteries although only a few would be able to retain the knowledge of its importance. They also knew that, eventually, *the circle and the handle of the ankh would reveal a heavenly invisible city that would work as a magnet to tie all the celestials, in human form, back together again.* They knew the ankh's symbol would help them reawaken and unveil the mysteries of spiritual gifts needed to prepare the Earth for the higher celestials who would come again. These higher celestials would assist in the setting up of a new government and the establishment of laws that would serve in creating the new world of peace.

Because the Mirror of Venus is actually the energy to help unveil the higher self of divine love and light, they knew some of them would be drawn to a particular "Four Corners" geographical location where the celestial energy's influence could best be utilized. However, although localized, they knew that the Mirror of Venus energy would trigger other high energy grid sites throughout the world in many locations. They knew it was a template of energy that could affect the entire planet and humanity's evolving consciousness.

So that you can better understand the potential power of this Four Corners area for light workers, I need to explain something called the four L's, and will now request that you pause a moment, please. **(See Illustration #6)**

Kindly take time to draw over this equilateral cross that looks like a large plus sign to experience its energy. Can you see that there are four L-shaped angles contained in the cross that meet in the center point? (Some of the L's are backward and upside down.)

Illustration #6 – The Equilateral Cross

The equilateral cross, as you call it, is a solar cross that holds the power of the Mirror of Venus because it contains the power of the four L's. These angles, or L's, identify the four stages of consciousness development that will open the doorways to the heavenly worlds needed to exit Earth. Please remember the four stages of consciousness as law, life, light and love.

1. Law—also called system and order. It is the law of the Great Balance that creates discipline. Without discipline you cannot have system and order. The word discipline contains the word disciple, which requires patience, commitment and the free will choice to be a disciple or practitioner of the law of balance.

2. Life—the vibratory level you are experiencing that is a spiritual expression of your true essence, which demonstrates your consciousness level. Life requires that you learn to live in the "now." As you accept being in the moment, everything else disappears. Then there is no longer a past or a future, only oneness or the present eternal circle of illumination.

3. Light—the ethereal understanding of the higher Self, or the resurrected body. Light is simply the vibration through which the Creator allows the gifts of power and the gifts of the mind to become manifested through a physical form. By using light, the process of changing from a dense physical body to a physical-etheric form can occur through the rearrangement of cellular levels to a higher molecular nature.

4. Love—Divine illumination. Love is the energy of being in the perfection of self as a co-creator with the Creator. Love is Oneness.

These four L's meet exactly where the right angles of America's four western states of Arizona, New Mexico, Utah and Colorado touch. While these four L's are easy to remember they may be somewhat challenging for humanity to model.

These four L's are also a representation of the four archangels and the four elements they express. So in the equilateral cross, the four L's explain how this world was created by those you call the archangels. It was created with the fire energy that I, the Archangel Michael, bring you from the Central Sun. It was also created by Archangel Raphael who is the over-viewer of the air, the breath, the oxygen. It was created by Archangel Uriel who brings the water, which is also the hydrogen, and which carries the unconscious. And it was created by Archangel Gabriel who holds the law of solidity and is presently rearranging the carbon element from the dust of the Earth to silicon, or crystal light energy. Your world is now changing its form into the element of resurrection and humanity knows it not.

Now I ask you to examine the physical areas contained within the Mirror of Venus map **(See Illustration #7, next page)** and notice whether you have lived in, or visited any of them. (There is no judgment if you have not.) Observe that there is an energy circle connected to an energetic handle that continues throughout Colorado, Wyoming, Idaho, and Montana, en route to Canada. *Please notice the dotted lines illustrating the extended area of influence.* The vibration of this handle is symbolic of my protective sword, and this sword holds the vibration of my blue flame.

Every person living within these areas is now under the Lemurian vibration that many of you once experienced long ago. This area is the only place within America where four states join together for the purposes of connecting the ancient symbol of the four L's. When this area's vortices have been activated, it will eventually activate all other major vortices throughout the rest of America, as well as the world. We are using the Four Corners, then, as a designated area of the United States for this symbol to represent the major influences of Law, Life, Light and Love. This specific area is simply where the Mirror of Venus is activating my transmutable blue flame and working as a magnet to draw all the star seeds, star lights, and star children back to that physical location where they had been before. (More about these groups shortly.)

My transmutable blue flame that is activating the Four Corners area now is inducing a higher frequency, which is

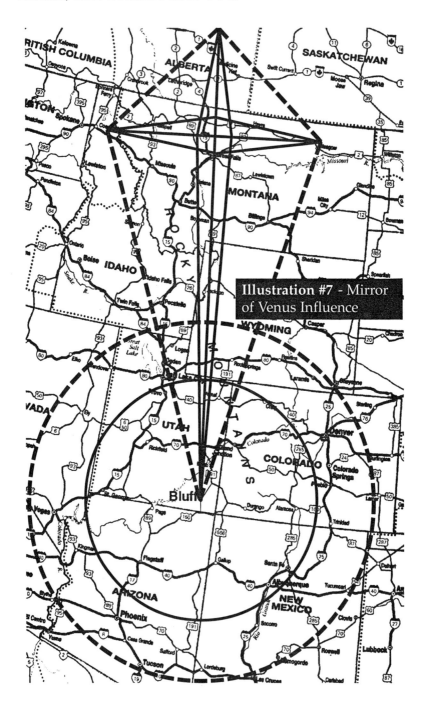

Illustration #7 - Mirror of Venus Influence

causing an invisible spiral to emanate from the hidden vibration of Law, Life, Light and Love. We are introducing the Mirror of Venus information for humanity to understand that the powerful Venusian and Lemurian vibrations are calling humanity to demonstrate their own applications of Law, Life, Light, and Love *now*!

The central part of the Mirror of Venus is in that intensified area where the four L's meet at the Four Corners area of Utah, Colorado, Arizona and New Mexico, and is contained within what we call the Electro-magnetic Gold Band of energy. **(See Illustration #8)**

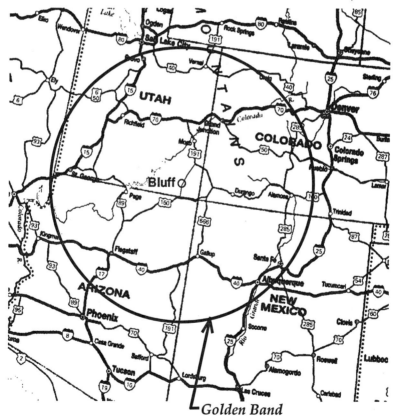

Illustration #8 - Four Corners Electro-magnetic Gold Band
Bluff, Utah is at the center of the band (circle).

It may assist you to think of the Mirror of Venus and the Four Corners maps as symbolic representations of an etheric city of light that is overshadowing the Four Corners area. This etheric city is currently sending telepathic thought to many of you who reside within these areas—or who may benefit from moving or visiting there. There are other developing light cities throughout your world, of course, but the Four Corners is specialized because where the corners of the four states meet, they form that energy cross of powerful geometrical influence called the four L's, already described.

Bluff, Utah is the heart center or pivotal point of the source of energy in the Electromagnetic Gold Band and is known as the generator. Because each of the four states within the Golden Band is under the etheric Overshadowing City, or circle of energy above it, special emphasis relating to the Lemurian fields of technology, education and healing are being highlighted. Those who live in, or will migrate to, the Four Corners area are the ancient Lemurians, and possibly some Atlanteans, coming back into the frequency that they had previously used in Venus and other stellar systems.

So this Lemurian vortex is being activated by a whirlwind of uplifted energy in the Four Corners area to work like a magnet drawing all those souls from long ago who will again awaken for the purpose of assisting through these greater times of change.

This Lemurian vortex in the Four Corners area is important because it connects to many other major sites and assists in the activation of all vortices throughout the world. However, I want to emphasize the vital role being played by Earth's Inner Worlds, spiritual beings, and dimensions you know so little about. There are hidden cities of light within and around your planet, generally unknown, whose entrances are accessible only through the many vortices within the mountainous regions. In the Four Corners area these regions include the Rocky Mountains, the Tetons, Mount Taylor, the San Francisco Peaks, the Superstition Mountains, Mingus Mountain, the White Mountains, the Valley of the

Gods, the Catalina Mountains, Wapatki, Sedona, and also the kivas and innumerable other ancient ruins. Many indigenous people such as the Anasazi, Hopi and Navaho Indians have lived in these areas to hold the knowledge and to maintain their spiritual integrity for all of humanity.

Now that you know more about the importance of Earth's grids and vortices, I want you to see how that knowledge helps your everyday life.

More and more circles of light are gathering and beginning to exchange their spiritual gifts and knowledge. They are learning how to express themselves and bring their thought into manifested form. Many of you are already teachers who are bringing education to many souls who do not yet know of these things. Some of you reading this material are the leaders and pioneers of kindred soul groups coming back together in these latter days to meet once again and to rekindle each other's gifts for the good of all life. When the star seeds, star lights and star children join together, the star colonies will actually begin to function on Earth once again. The gathering of these many like-minded humans such as those within the Mirror of Venus and the Four Corners area will recreate a joyous and cooperative way of life.

As I define these terms of "star seeds," "star lights," and "star children," I ask you to remember that there is no judgment about who is better, more valuable, or more loved. All beings have the Golden Ray of Cosmic Consciousness within and are proceeding at their own free will pace of growth. What is important to understand is that because you have had different experiences, you will have different interests and abilities. All we ask of you is that you seek to practice spiritual Law, Life, Light, and Love at your highest level of dedication. From such an energy of commitment all that you give and share will automatically take you where God would have you be.

STAR SEEDS

All those souls presently embodied on the Earth who

chose to come from other interplanetary systems, higher worlds or spheres are called star seeds. These star seeds are celestial beings who incarnated on Earth eons ago. This happened at the time of pre-dynasty Egypt when many descended into the vibration of human frequency because they wanted to experience emotion and feeling through living in a physical form. Some other star seeds deliberately came through "The Doors of Sacrifice," which means they chose to stay on Earth in order to assist in the upliftment of those caught in the illusion of duality.

STAR LIGHTS

Those we call star lights, or earthlings, are those souls who have never experienced life elsewhere in the Cosmos or on any other planetary system. The star lights first began life on the Earth plane through evolution's path and have not yet evolved to a state of consciousness high enough to pass through the doors of illusion. Most star lights have incarnated over many life experiences, however, and have been schooled by the star seeds who have brought new teachings in order to uplift their consciousness. The star lights are now awakening and are preparing for their next higher education.

STAR CHILDREN

Star children are those beings coming into your Earth plane from the higher schools of thought and existence. They come from celestial realms like Venus, Jupiter, Pleiades, Sirius, Andromeda, Arcturus, Böötes, Mazzaroth, Ratoema and many more. These beings began incarnating about 30,000 years ago, most especially since the dynasties of Egypt, but they have not experienced as many Earth incarnations as the star seeds have. However, the influence of star children has greatly increased since the 1960's.

Their specific purpose is to create the New Age, the Peaceful Millennium, or Golden Dawn. Many of these souls are incredibly sensitive, artistic, and have extraordinary minds. You sometimes call them prodigies or gifted children, for they are very ingenious in the areas of science, philosophy, mathematics, technology, art, music, politics, the social and ecological fields, health, and so forth.

They have also come to Earth knowing that they are different and most don't agree with "the system" as it presently exists. Many keep to themselves because they have a feeling that they must stay focused in order to change some aspect of the world. Some of these children also have incredible gifts of the mind, of telepathy, of kinetic powers, and of hearing and receiving knowledge from the higher guardians who have brought them here to help create the divine plan on Earth.

Unfortunately, some star children may find Earth life such an enormous challenge that they become angry, frustrated, disappointed, and "drop out" of the established cultures. These star children need special guidance to help them to fulfill their unique soul purposes and I ask you to foster their consciousness with your caring and love.

As previously mentioned, many of the angelic forces—the Ascended Masters, the higher intelligences, and the robed ones—are working diligently in Earth's Inner Worlds and vortices to prepare you telepathically to uncover your cosmic memory and thoughts of inspiration. This contact will help you in creating new spiritual centers in such places as the Four Corners area and many other locations. In future days, many individuals will seek the help of these centers in order to learn how to stay centered and balanced as the Earth goes through its geological, political, economic, and ecological changes.

In time, as you further awaken, you will help uplift the collective consciousness of humanity. It is in your power to teach them to hold steadfast through the greater changes that will occur on Earth and begin the glorious era called the Peaceful Millennium, New Age, or Golden Dawn.

Now I will pause and ask for your questions, Virginia.

* * *

VE: Greetings to you once again, and thank you for your fascinating discussion. My first question is this. How many light centers do we need in the Mirror of Venus and the Four Corners area to really take advantage of these energies?

AM: There is an Overshadowing City—which I shall explain more fully in the next chapter—and its energy is primarily positioned over three major centers in each state, making a total of 12 energized centers. The 13th energy center is near the heart chakra point at Bluff, Utah.

VE: Does this mean there can only be three centers in each of the four states?

AM: Yes, for the major sites, but it can really be multiples of 12. There will be many centers located throughout the four states, inter-connecting geometrically something like a spider web.

VE: Is there any particular time line for when these centers should start?

AM: They have already started, beloved one, and will continue to advance through the year of 2012. Then even greater works will begin.

VE: Have most of the light workers, who were called to populate the Mirror of Venus area for this time of awakening, appeared in that region yet?

AM: Many have done so beginning about 1986 and most particularly since Halley's Comet's last passing. The comet brought in the blue flame that inter-penetrated and opened more of Earth's Inner World portals. The rays hit the center of the planet and then bounced out into the human subtle body fields. This assisted in the awakening process near the time that some called the Harmonic Convergence.

Just as there is still a migration into the Four Corners area, small groups are also forming in other areas of the Mirror of Venus within my sword of protection.

VE: What other U.S. areas beside the Four Corners and the Mirror of Venus are already developing in order to support what's happening here in the Four Corners? What are the main regions outside of the U.S.?

AM: I have chosen to use the Mirror of Venus for an

example because it is the only place where four states bound-aries come together in the form of a cross utilizing the four L's already described. However, there are many centers of light that are building throughout the U.S., and also throughout the whole world. Remember light is gathering light, as dark-ness is gathering its momentum of darkness. All souls who are ready, regardless of age, race, gender, creed or color, will drop their negative belief systems and come back into the Oneness. They will recognize and respect each other re-gardless of religion and join together in the name of love to create peace. This is not limited to the Four Corners. Many will become illuminators.

I will briefly mention a few important states in America as well as some international locations. There are major devel-opments in California, Florida, Hawaii, Missouri, Montana, North Carolina, Oklahoma, Virginia and Washington parti-cularly. Places such as Australia, Canada, Egypt, England, France, India, Israel, Peru, and Russia are important interna-tionally. My blue flame is being sent throughout the whole of your world, but there are definite geographical locations and countries that I am using as major activating stations. Western Canada holds my vibration of the blue flame and my flame is also very connected to Israel as another major country of importance.

As the greater activity begins, and people energetically create and teach in their schools and centers, this positive change will activate the ley lines that will then create a ripple effect not only in the U.S. but throughout the world when the time is ready. The grids and ley lines, the vortices, and your own energies are also connected to many of the systems of light throughout your solar system. They will all work together for gathering light. Know that we are your stalwart companions who assist in this powerful consciousness shift and who are preparing the magnificent world of light awaiting your presence.

Squares represent
cubes

3 Cities, 3 Gates

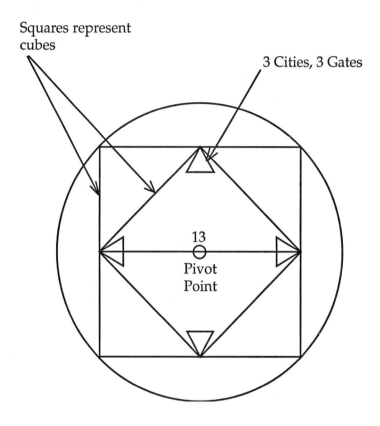

13
Pivot
Point

Illustration #9 - The Overshadowing City over the Four
Corners Area of the United States

> If you knew that sacred geometry would raise
> the spiritual vibration of your buildings, would
> you dare experiment with new designs?

Chapter 3

The Overshadowing City

When looking at this Overshadowing City illustration **(See Illustration #9, previous page)** please note that this huge etheric city of light is composed of twelve smaller cities grouped within four triangles that each hold three cities or centers making a total of twelve. Then observe that there are two squares, which represent two cubes, each cube having six walls for a total of twelve. Each of the twelve walls has a different inlaid gem and color that imparts unique vibrations to the energy of the Overshadowing City.

At the pivot point in the center of the drawing is the number 13. This powerful number 13 opens a path or gateway to both Earth's Inner Worlds and also to the celestial dimensions. This follows the pattern of Jesus the Christ who appointed himself 12 disciples because he embodied the light and power of the number 13, which symbolized the path between worlds. It was this path, this way, that he shared with his disciples so they might uplift into their higher evolution.

In your earthly Bible, in Revelation 21:10-22, you will notice that humanity was given a description of an architectural design used in the creation of the holy city called the "New Jerusalem." Because there are various biblical versions and different interpretations of what Revelation states, rather than printing one of them as the correct version, let me just synthesize a simple statement to focus on what all versions contain.

The New Jerusalem is described as being laid four square and within the wall (square) the city has 12 foundations, 12 gates, 12 crystals and the 12 tribes of Israel.

You may find Revelation 21:10-22 rather complicated or confusing, but there is great value in comprehending the fact that it represents a description of a geometrical design that, when understood, can be used for the betterment of humanity's daily life and spiritual evolution. Although the existing New Jerusalem city described in the Bible will *not* descend over the entire planet Earth until the time of ascension, you are being given a smaller replica over the Four Corners area now to accelerate the Earth's grid and raise human consciousness. This influence is a wonderful gift that should send your spirit soaring!

I say again that our hovering angelic city over the Four Corners area is only a forerunner or model of the unspeakably wondrous celestial city, the New Jerusalem, that will one day encompass the entire planet. Nevertheless, our smaller angelic city is vital to your current lives. We call this angelic location the Overshadowing City because it holds an enormous group of inter-dimensional beings from multiple cosmic systems whose prime mission is to positively influence the Earth and human consciousness. Though you may not realize it, we have several ways to help you from this angelic city's position.

The first way in which we are assisting you is by telepathic contact through our supportive thoughts. We intend to provide inspiration and encouragement to help you to unveil your latent abilities—just as many other celestial beings are doing.

The second way we seek to serve you is by clarifying the importance of the Earth's Inner World cities and by explaining their connection to you. We hope to awaken your willingness to influence your architects to design your new buildings with certain geometrical plans containing crystals that will help you utilize the information and inspiration emanating from both Earth's Inner World cities and the celestial realms. You see, you are very important to your own graduation and ascension! And our suggested geometrically designed buildings and centers with inlaid crystals will accelerate your awakening and safe participation in the coming times. These inlaid crystal patterns in your buildings are of vital importance to you because they energize, balance and create an electro-magnetic connection, or labyrinth, with other centers on Earth utilizing the same geometric principles.

This connection is critical in providing the stepping stones for the creation of a higher human consciousness needed to achieve a more cooperative and powerful way of life. Just imagine! *Through your cooperation in building these designs you will receive crystal transmissions from both the physical-etheric position of the Overshadowing City and also those energies radiating from within the Earth's Inner Worlds. For the first time in thousands of years you can be consciously absorbing Earth's own inner spiritual energies and those of the Cosmos simultaneously. It is a wondrous and exciting experience not to be missed.*

GRID FORMULA FOR BUILDINGS

Although I have focused on the importance of the Four Corners energy pattern in America, be assured there is a geometrical formula for homes, centers, and buildings that connects people anywhere on the planet to both the higher heavens and to the Earth's Inner Worlds. No one who loves God is left out! The reason constructing buildings in this particular geometrical pattern is desirable is that these geometrical formulas facilitate the raising of consciousness for the humans inside these dwellings. This higher frequency helps people to unveil or reveal their innate spiritual gifts and abilities—which is why you chose to be on Earth at this unique time.

I am going to describe this basic geometrical formula and

present several designs helpful in the building of your centers, schools, and homes. But first I need to clarify some simple mathematical information for you concerning the number 9. This number 9 connects into the higher vibration of divine light that is the universal love of the trinity. You might say it is a holy number.

Numbers are the sacred science of vibration or the language of God. Man, the primate, didn't have any knowledge of mathematics so it had to be introduced by the celestials. On your planet there are only nine numbers—1,2,3,4,5,6,7,8,9— plus the 0 or cipher. Humanity's whole reality is therefore based upon the energy vibration of these few numbers in relationship to one another.

The sacred science of vibration has always been recognized as the key to wisdom and was taught in early mystery schools to carefully selected initiates. For you today, however, I simply want to focus on the value of the sacred number 9 as expressed in the sequence of $144,000 = (1+4+4+0+0+0) = 9$

All of the geometrical designs for your buildings must be used with the mathematical number of 144,000 because *the number 144,000—which is a 9 (1+4+4=9)— represents completion and universal love. Therefore, this 144,000 equation is the only one to be used in plotting the amount of square footage or acreage needed to connect with both Earth's Inner Worlds and the higher celestial worlds*

Please understand that the size of the land or acreage you build on should follow this formula using the number 144,000. You can select the appropriate land size for your purposes according to these recommendations.

3.31 acres = 144,000 sq. ft.
5.51 acres = 288,999 sq. ft. (2+8+8+9+9+9=45; 4+5=9)
9.93 acres = 432,000 sq. ft. (4+3+2=9)
13.23 acres = 576,000 sq. ft. (5+7+6=18; 1+8=9)
16.55 acres = 720,000 sq. ft. (7+2=9)

Any larger sites follow the same formula.

Even if finances or land availability make it impossible to

find a 3.31 acre piece of land, you can still participate in building your home or center by following the recommended geometrical formula. This basic formula utilizes the square, triangle, and circle because it creates a geometric pattern wherever the lines and angles connect together. When the lines join together they create a specific pattern of energy, which in turn creates a vibratory blueprint that links to a spider web system of light, multiple colors and sound.

These three common geometrical symbols—the square, triangle and circle—are explained this way:

Square: The square represents the Earth, density and matter. These squares also connect to other geographical locations or major sites within the grid lines. The square symbolizes earthly solidity upon which your edifices are being built, as well as the concrete material actually used for their construction.

Triangle: The lines of the triangle represent the ley lines connecting to the Inner Worlds or to hidden dimensions within the Earth that hold a higher frequency. These are entered through the mountains, kivas, ancient ruins, desert floors, subterranean entrances and megalithic and monolithic structures.

Circle: The circle represents a band of energy that connects to the higher celestial realms, the Universe and the greater Omniverse worlds. Because it is whole and undivided the circle also represents Oneness or the Golden Circle of Eternal Breath.

The energy grids of the Overshadowing City will benefit you only if you build your earthly structures in its exact pattern. **(See Illustration #10, next page)** Notice in the middle of the circle there is a pivot point that acts as the heart chakra, which is the number 13 or the pathway of celestial energy. The pivot point connects to the 12 dwellings located within the 4 triangles; so each triangle has 3 dwellings. In each of the triangles you can build your homes in a number of different architectural designs. In other words you are free to select any design for your personal homes as long as the buildings are

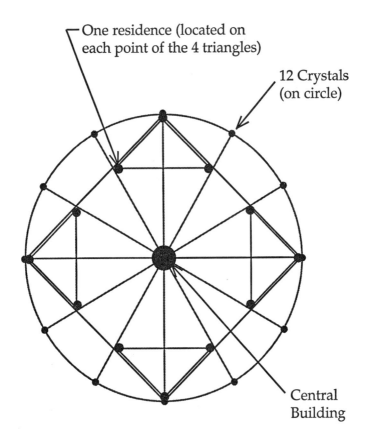

One residence (located on each point of the 4 triangles)

12 Crystals (on circle)

Central Building

Illustration # 10 – Basic Grid Design for Utilizing the Overshadowing City's Energy

placed within the triangle formations located inside the square.

The lines within the square can be walkways or bridges connecting twelve homes to the pivot point of the circle's center which will be the main edifice and can have many different styles of single or multiple levels. Each group will decide on their own purpose and develop the compatible relationships necessary to achieve it. Some centers will be simple, others grandiose. For example, a large three-story dome could have the bottom portion as meeting places, lecture halls, eating facilities, and offices. The second floor could contain various classes for education, healing, technology and other subjects. The third or top floor could be the meditation room for various individuals or groups to connect with spirit, through silence, to awaken love for self, for God and all of life. But of course your central building's size must meet your own group's needs and purposes.

In certain religious groups the living quarters and churches or temples are combined together, providing the potential for a high state of consciousness to be achieved. However, fewer people seek such situations today, and contemporary society members need additional opportunities to connect themselves with the Peaceful Millennium's energy and guidance.

Some of you hunger for community and relationships with your spiritual brothers and sisters. You dream of a new world and long for the fulfillment of God's plan on Earth. I offer you support of that dream by this information which explains one way you can build your homes, schools, your community and spiritual meeting places. There are new ideas arising about community living, and many of you are drawn to express yourselves in such patterns as co-housing or shared living quarters. This Overshadowing City plan advances those ideas by deliberately inserting geometrical patterns and crystalline stones within your homes and centers in order to connect with specific spiritual support much needed during these challenging times.

You may remember I briefly discussed the biblical references to the New Jerusalem contained in Revelation 21. In that description of the New Jerusalem city there were 12 crystals or precious stones laid within its walls. Today on Earth you can use these described crystals or precious stones to your own advantage in the homes and buildings you erect, in order to balance the property grid upon which you live.

Do you know the names of these twelve precious stones/

crystals? They are called Jasper, Sapphire, Chalcedony, Emerald, Sardonyx, Sardiums, Chrysolite, Beryl, Chrysoprasus, Jacinth and Amethyst. Remember that because of the present density of Earth, they may not seem very crystalline or vibrant. However, in Lemurian days and in the higher dimensions now these shimmering crystal stones hold volumes of incredible knowledge useful in raising the vibration of individuals and the collective consciousness. If you cannot obtain these specific stones, you can use stones/minerals of the same color that will hold a similar but less powerful composite of energy.

The basic color of each stone/crystal is as follows:

Jasper—opaque red; **Sapphire**—blue; **Chalcedony**—translucent grayish or milky quartz; **Emerald**—green; **Sardonyx**—white chalcedony and the sard which is reddish brown chalcedony; **Sardius**—red ruby chalcedony; **Chrysolite**—olivine or any group of magnesium, iron or silicates; **Beryl**—green, blue, white, rose and golden, both opaque and transparent; **Topaz**—citrine, pale yellow, lemon, translucent variety of quartz; **Chrysoprasus**—a green variety of chalcedony; **Jacinth**—hyacinth a reddish-orange zircon; and **Amethyst**—purple or violet quartz.

These 12 stones which were mentioned in Revelation 21 are truly needed on Earth today in certain precise patterns because of their vibrations and conductivity. Aaron's breastplate, for example, which used these 12 stones, was actually a communication device worn on his physical body that brought him into higher wisdom.

Now that you know the types of stones/crystals needed, you may be wondering how many to obtain and where to put them. This depends on the type of center you are building. From the very beginning of the planning stages, the designers must follow the geometrical formula, including the placement of the inlaid crystals. In the initial planning of the blueprint a harmonic agreement must be achieved so that a total comprehension of the final outcome, identifying all aspects needed to accomplish the finest grid patterns, is fulfilled.

As you refer back to the illustration, look at the center's pivot point and imagine a dwelling upon it. This building must have all 12 stones/crystals (or increments of 12, 24, 36) inlaid in its walls, in the foundation, or buried underground so its energy will connect to the 12 stones/crystals placed on the diameter of the circle. It is on each of these 12 locations— represented by small black dots—that you place one of the 12 different stones/crystals so that one of each kind has been individually placed around the circle without duplication. Depending on the size of the stones/crystals that you can obtain, you can even place all 12 stones on each of the 12 sites, expanding to the power of 144 (1 + 4 + 4 = 9). Through any of these placements you will have created an invisible energy field.

Kindly observe the large square containing 4 triangles. Each triangle holds 3 buildings for a total of 12 inside the square. Each of the 12 buildings, represented by the large black dots, must have one of the 12 different stones/crystals without duplication, or each of the 12 building sites can contain all 12 stones.

As you study this illustration of the Overshadowing City, remember that the precision in duplicating this plan is critical to the geometrical formula's success because it creates an invisible kaleidoscope of color, sound and melodious tones which energetically connects you with the Earth and the Cosmos.

In addition to this basic pattern, I will now discuss an alternative grid design for utilizing the Overshadowing City's energy that will also be acceptable. Please note that this pattern is still utilizing the same three basic geometrical symbols of the circle, square and the triangle (There may be other acceptable patterns as well—as long as you use these three basic symbols). **(See Illustration #11, next page)** Once again when you have decided how large you want the building in the

Pastures or Agriculture
(between square & circle)

Courtyards
(within
inner circle)

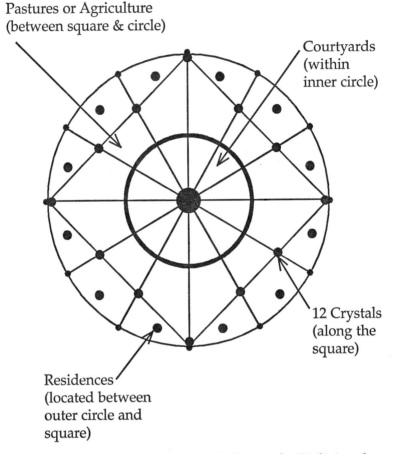

12 Crystals
(along the
square)

Residences
(located between
outer circle and
square)

Illustration #11 - Alternate Grid Design for Utilizing the
Overshadowing City's Energy

pivot point center to be, you must decide, according to its
size, whether you want a minimum of 12 stones/crystals or if
you want multiples of 12, such as 24, 36, or larger.

The small circle drawn around the pivot point in the center
represents an area that can be used to beautify a courtyard,
used for general landscaping, or for other esthetic purposes.

There are other places in this design that you can use
stones/crystals. Where the black dots are located on the

square, and also on the outside diameter of the large circle, you can place another 24 stones/crystals. This is because the circle has its own 12 locations—represented by the small black dots. Where the 4 points of the square meet the circle, each corner of the square will require 2 crystals, 1 for the circle and 1 for the square.

You will have to calculate the exact measurements of the outer circle's 12 divine triangles (pie-shaped sections) that connect to the pivot point in the center. Notice that these 12 triangles each have one dwelling exactly placed in the center of the triangle near the outer circle as shown by the large black dots. These 12 living quarters will each have all 12 major stones/crystals inlaid at the base of each entrance, in the foundation itself, or even above ground inside or outside the home. As long as the pattern utilizes the energy of the number 12, or any increment of 12 such as 24, 36, etc., you can place as many stones/crystals as your body can safely tolerate. Dowsing may assist you in determining the correct number of stones/crystals needed and is recommended as a tool for light workers. (Note: For information about dowsing contact the American Society of Dowsers, Inc., PO Box 24, Danville, VT 05828)

May I remind you again that the energy maintained within your pivot point centers and homes can change according to their location, the architectural blueprints, your own consciousness and the group's efforts. This is because the various designs will hold different patterns of energy according to how the angles are placed together in the grid design. That is why the soul groups who choose to find each other and decide to build a center will stay together only if their vibration remains harmonious to the grid's energy.

Although the grids are invisible, they have musical symphony chords resonating in a higher language or frequency. This wonderful frequency inspires humanity to express their talents and gifts of spirit through manifested ideas and actions. When a person's harmonic vibration is incompatible with the higher frequencies of the grid the person will grow restless, or even begin to display irritation and want to move on.

Only some of the star seeds, star children and star lights are being motivated to build centers, schools, and homes in these designs. Others may feel drawn to enter into these centers for learning and teaching once they are built. Some people must physically migrate in order to meet their own kindred soul groups, or find the cosmic families that they agreed to reunite with long ago in the inner pyramids of early Egypt. Not all of you will have the availability to participate in these centers or visit major sites throughout your country or the world, but you may still connect to each center or vortex through the telepathic power of your mind through meditation. You can also create vortices in your homes, or backyards, by sitting inside a circle of crystals, by creating labyrinths, geometrical grids, medicine wheels or by chanting, singing and listening to musical tones that will also connect you into the major grids.

These spiritual activities create energies that will connect to the invisible ley lines of the grids allowing some people to travel via their light body. It may also be possible to connect to the major vortices where everyone will have their own individual experience according to their own level of evolvement.

You do not have to go to any particular vortex unless you feel strongly motivated to do so. However, if you are guided to a major site, you could have a unique experience connected with that one particular vortex. This association with the energy sometimes opens the doors to a past life experience that could unveil certain memories, or assure a contact with one particular individual or other like-minded associates. If you find yourself being motivated to visit a particular vortex, a spiritual awakening could occur that may enhance your development. When you enter into a sacred vortex you could possibly experience differences in breathing patterns, energy tremors, pain in different areas of the body or an out-of-body event. If this occurs, it's because you wanted to revisit an area in order to decode a particular memory that would bring you into a greater awakening of self.

There are many people who have already built their own centers and are using different patterns of living and working in both structured and unstructured ways. Some people are called to return to the land to grow organic food and live more natural lives while others are guided to create other constructive enterprises. These centers will express many different purposes and may be used for refuge in order to help many people on Earth during the future challenges and changes.

I have presented two suggested patterns for your various centers so you may coalesce into a spiritual community for the experience of joy, comradeship, service and evolution. As free will creations, of course, you must decide what is appropriate for you. In the simplest of terms, however, such group endeavors can provide the experience of feeling at home in physical life until you return to a higher dimension.

Now let me pause here, Virginia, to ask if you have any questions.

* * *

VE: Greetings once again, and thank you so much for sharing these intriguing thoughts with us. Would you please describe something more about the Overshadowing City? How long has it been there? Who started it? What is the energy source used to assist us in our geometrically designed inlaid crystal buildings?

AM: You are asking for a description about another dimension, but I will gladly give a further understanding. The Overshadowing City is another system of light within your Universe that has always existed, but it was first repositioned over the Four Corners area during the time of Lemuria and early Egypt. However, it was not intended to be used or activated in assisting the star seeds, star lights, and star children until they were mature enough to open their memories of the prior crystal civilization. In your world you would understand this to be about fifty years ago when mankind began to utilize the higher scientific technologies.

The Overshadowing City is comprised of many different timekeepers and executives from the celestial spheres of your solar system. Our source of power utilizes electro-magnetic and bio-gravitational fields of energy.

VE: Thank you. Could you give us some idea of what our lives will be like when we start using your recommended geometrical formula with the inlaid stones/crystals?

AM: For many years upon the Earth, for the purposes of learning and growth, there has been a low frequency that has held both Earth and humanity in density. However, your Earth is spinning into a higher frequency, and those who are awakening will begin to release that limiting density. Many of your present buildings have been designed utilizing the square, which is the symbol of density or solidity. So as the Earth is changing her frequency, it is advisable for humans to change the shape of the structures they live and work in by using the mathematical higher frequencies contained in the triangle, circles or half circles called arches. I realize that not everyone can change their physical structures. However, you can begin to utilize the geometry of these designs within your homes and centers to assist in raising the vibration where you spend most of your personal time.

For example, as I said before, if you take a square and put it on a mechanism that can spin it into a high frequency, the square rearranges itself into a circle. This same analogy applies to the designing of your many different buildings, homes, temples and churches. The square, by itself, is an energy limitation or suppressant, whereas the circle will open you to the frequencies of the spheric worlds. The triangle will take you deep within yourself to unfold the greater mysteries of soul and connect you to the Earth's Inner Worlds.

The stones/crystals will energetically assist you in creating a higher frequency for living within physical structures. This will aid in helping you to unveil latent abilities and to open memories of your spiritual gifts, such as using higher levels of telepathic communication in order to receive messages from the celestial kingdoms.

You may also advance in the techniques of remote viewing, psycho-kinetic abilities, receiving visions, enhancing healing techniques, using mind power abilities, and developing technology to protect yourselves from negative political, economical, and ecological situations. Many of your artists and musicians will be bringing a higher language from the Universe to assist in the use of the colors and tones to help open the soul memory.

All of this is to help humanity to awaken, to assist with new laws and philosophies, and to keep yourself and others balanced as the physical world about you continues to go through its necessary changes.

VE: Great! So how much higher do our personal vibratory energies need to increase before we can safely utilize these incoming energies and not get emotionally unbalanced? Tell us more about how our coming together again fulfills those prior commitments and soul purposes.

AM: In the time of early Egypt, the celestial beings placed all they knew in a "fail-safe" system, (Akashic record) to be coded and decoded (memories awakened) at an appropriate time. Doing this would advance themselves, and also assist humanity, because the soul would know exactly the moment when this memory could be safely released to allow these divine abilities to come forth. At that time, in their wisdom, each of the star seeds chose to give some of their abilities to be kept by another star seed in their cosmic group, and vice-versa. This assured that when the memories began to open, they would meet each other at the appropriate time of maturity and give each other the missing pieces.

Today, there are many who are working on projects throughout Earth, be it healing, education, or technology, who feel that they have greater knowing and solutions, but can't quite put it all together. That is because they haven't found their counterparts with whom they planned to meet. So some of you have gifts to receive and also to impart. When you meet now, both beings will have matured enough to safely release the knowledge. This was done purposely, for protection, to avoid misusing former power. As you continue to trust your guidance, your energies will become higher and more evenly balanced. Some of you will miraculously and synchronisticly come together if you truly wish to be reunited.

At the same time the humans who experience imbalance are those holding onto the old belief systems that keep them imprisoned in density. These people will feel emotional, distraught, angry, frustrated and lost, because they haven't let the God source within them advance into the higher frequencies of graduated change. That is why many of the illuminators must wake up in order to learn to maintain a balance and calmness. You are needed to be the beacons of light to help many others who will be confused as these changes occur. You are needed to nurture, to give love, and to help the confused regain their equilibrium.

VE: Thank you so much for describing these helpful building designs! I have noticed that other channels are currently recommending many different kinds of building plans that are somewhat different from yours. Will those different plans all be compatible or is it going to be confusing?

AM: Different types will not be confusing, Virginia, because all styles of patterns used for buildings still connect into the divine circle. The design that I have given is valuable because it can be rearranged in multiple patterns. The power is within the angles. As the angles are formulated together, this connects each line or angle into the universal language of color, light and sound via the invisible lines that create a grid. There is not one single design that isn't at least some part of the recommended geometrical pattern. Even the square can be divided into the four or more triangles. I have given you a basic model and several ways you can utilize this geometrical coding system. Depending on the design as a whole, and the way the angles connect, it can hold a higher or lower energy. Any choice you make will be educational.

VE: Sounds good. Can you recommend any particular building materials that would be best suited for building our new or adapted centers and homes?

AM: If you could build utilizing crystals or materials that are transparent, then this would hold a greater vibratory rate. Many of the celestial cities in your solar system are angelic realms created out of gold, precious gems, and fire crystals. They have the capacity to hold and reflect the greater power of the Sun's source. Since humanity isn't sufficiently developed yet to use the techniques needed to create in this manner, I have given you information about the geometrical designs and the placement of stones/crystals that connect into these higher vibratory frequencies.

As to the favorite type of building products, you can use any material such as steel, iron, aluminum, concrete, earth, straw bales, tires, rocks or glass. Utilizing some forms and shapes of copper artistically placed also assists as a conductor of energy. Simply apply your creativity to the geometrical formula's principles, using the inlaid stones/crystals, and this will connect you to the higher frequencies that you desire.

VE: So if we are going to build a home using one of the recommended designs, does it have to have a minimum size in order to take advantage of these incoming energies?

AM: The size does not matter, only the design in which it is built. That means many people can participate.

VE: That's good news. Since there are many other places in Earth's Inner Worlds and in the higher spiritual realms, such as Shambala, how is the Overshadowing City's energy going to relate to them?

AM: These various planes of which you speak, such as Shambala, Shangri-la, Avalon and others are connected to Earth's Inner World dimensions, with experiences at their own level of development, but are not presently connected to the Earth as they once were. The Overshadowing City has been placed above the Earth plane to assist in the uplifting of humanity's consciousness and to bring the new world of peace.

Now I want to share more about your wonderful planet Earth's unique qualities that assist you in reaching higher levels of spiritual growth and consciousness.

Chapter 4

Your Life on Earth with the Harmonic Grids

Now that you know something of Earth's grids and vortices, the Mirror of Venus and the Four Corners area, and the importance of the Overshadowing City, it is time to pause and reflect upon how these various energies effect your physical and subtle energy bodies. Of course, many great thinkers and spiritual teachers have already explained what life is, and who humans are, from their perspective. Today I would like to share my own thoughts on these topics with you.

For your third dimension, life is the vitality of energy that expresses, experiments with and experiences matter by allowing the soul to formulate a physical body or organism composed of fire, air, earth and water. These four are the necessary elements that encompass your physical embodiment and your physical, mental and emotional states of being. Your bodies must have the four elements to survive or physical death occurs. Do you know how these four elements work in your body?

Let me begin with nitrogen/fire, which provides the electrical currents that create the positive and negative charges through the brain to activate the involuntary and voluntary nervous system. It is these currents that operate the brain components and the life force pulsation that keeps the heart pulsating in a rhythmic beat.

Oxygen/air is another essential element of the body, because the lungs must express the prana or life force energy in order for the heart to electrically pump that life energy through the grid system of the bloodstream's veins and arteries and the body's meridian system.

The element of hydrogen/water is the largest energy component of which your bodies are made, and it keeps all other elements in balance. Hydrogen also acts as a conductor of all the body's energy, and is the carrier of unconscious thought. It is through the bloodstream that all genetic coding is nourished. Lastly, you have the element of carbon/matter, which is the structured shell or housing of your physical dense body in which all the cellular memories are stored.

Your main terminal for conducting life through your physical bodies is the brain. The brain is held together by matter/solid mass, and it cushions itself in hydrogen/liquid. It must have oxygen in order to exist so that the fire elements of positive and negative charges activate or initiate the brain power into action. Without these several elements and their inter-relationships no vehicle of matter can function.

You have the same elements within you that make up the Earth Mother. The nitrogen/fire element of Earth comes from the power of your local Sun. Through the Sun's particles of electro-magnetic energy Earth is nurtured, healed, and maintained. The oxygen/air of her lungs maintains a life force energy as breath for her life to be fully experienced. Earth's hydrogen/water is provided by the many oceans, seas, lakes and rivers. Her carbon/matter structure is made up of the dense mountain zones and the many minerals that are the marrow of her bones.

Your Earth was created by the higher celestials to express the law of duality, which required the use of these four elements of fire, air, earth and water. In ways mysterious to you, these elements create your plane of expression and each of these four elements are overseen by the four Archangels.

Nitrogen/fire: I, the Archangel Michael, am the overseer of fire, nitrogen, proton, electron, neutron, infrared rays, gamma rays and electromagnetic fields of energy. I carry the sword of truth, which is a rod of fire/light that overcomes and transmutes all darkness and negativity and brings the polarities of duality back into Oneness. Fire is a particle that comes from the Central Sun, and its influence interconnects with all the suns of light throughout space, beyond time and timelessness. God, or this light called the Flower of Fire, knows every act, deed, and thought throughout all realms of creation.

Oxygen/air: The Archangel Raphael is the overseer of the element of oxygen. Within its composition oxygen holds various levels of prana or life force called breath. Breath can be experienced in various stages which allows the physical, mental and emotional bodies to transmute negativity. Through breathing practices the physical body can change its rate of frequency by relaxing the brain's everyday Beta wave into a less stressful Alpha wave frequency. This shift releases the physical world's demands and opens the doorway to the inner kingdom. The power of breath can be utilized to take you into other worlds, dimensions and higher levels of knowledge.

Hydrogen/water: The Archangel Uriel is the overseer of this element. Hydrogen carries the potential of using the human unconscious in positive ways. When used positively, hydrogen brings an awakening and the renewal of spiritual awareness. Drinking pure water can cleanse the toxicity from the physical body. Humans find great joy in immersing themselves in water, or by being near it in its many forms. The negative ions from flowing water sources can energize and rejuvenate the body or provide relaxation and connection with spirit.

Carbon/matter: The Archangel Gabriel is the overseer of this element. Gabriel has been responsible for Earth's great abundance to humanity as well as her soul-inspiring beauty. Earth provides all of humanity's needs! From her air, water and soil come everything needed for human survival. Gabriel is heralding the great news that he is re-arranging the density of carbon/matter to silicon/crystal—and eventually to christos/light. This means the Earth plane is now spinning into a higher orbital frequency and the time will soon come when Earth will no longer stay in her dense dimension. Earth is accelerating and will be arising to meet the higher worlds.

To arise into the higher worlds with Earth, every person has had four invisible communications center given them at physical birth. These four communication centers were placed in them through the genetic coding of their physical, mental and emotional bodies. These four internal communication centers connect to the spiritual self, and as one develops, these internal centers are allowed to open and express. Positive thoughts and actions raise the kundalini fire, which activates your telepathic communication centers and releases the higher knowledge of the spiritual self. These communication centers are physical, but they are connected to the subtle auric fields of the body, as well. Here are the four specific positions of the body's communication centers.

The first communication center is located at the base of the spine and was used when humankind first walked the Earth in the early primitive era. In Neanderthal man the first communication was opened and this was called the "fight or flight" syndrome. These beings would receive a sense of danger and that would alert them to an instant reaction. Sometimes they would run to avoid the danger and other times they would stay and face it.

The second communication center is located in the abdominal brain or what you call the solar plexus. It is the seat of lower intuition, and this is the center that most humans are presently using at this time. We often hear you say that you had a "gut feeling" about something. Intuition is the feeling of knowing what to do. It is the voice from deep within guiding you to listen to useful information and direction. Today many humans are developing spiritually—thus they are starting to use their third communication center.

The third communication center is located just above the back of the neck and is called the medulla oblongata. It connects you into a mind-mind communication called telepathy. When this center opens you can retrieve information from the higher celestial planes of existence and unveil latent abilities according to your particular spiritual development.

The fourth communication center is located in the pituitary and pineal glands, which connect you to a telepathic language called soul-to-soul. It will take time for humanity to fully utilize this form of telepathic thought. There have been a few who have lived on Earth who were able to tap into this high communication center. Their ability was very limited, however, except for your greatest masters and lords of light. This center will be used more actively when soul aspects have passed through the veil of the 5th dimensional ascension and are then progressing through the 6th and 7th worlds of spirit and soul dimensions.

I recognize that the Earth's school is not easy, but the Father/Mother God does hold it in great appreciation. For those who have chosen to incarnate on Earth and go through the various tests of life after life in order to perfect their purposes, their spiritual growth will be an exponential accomplishment. Therefore, I ask you to use your God-given communication centers wisely and deliberately!

Though you may not remember it now, before you were born into a physical body your soul specifically chose the correct energy places on the planet it needed to best activate its purposes and intentions for this current lifetime. So even before earthly life began you had already made a blueprint that contained one or more physical locations best suited for the completion of your life purposes. Your soul did this because Earth contains many vortices that hold particular harmonic chord frequencies, and it wanted to be physically situated to absorb these particular energies and influences. Much as humans choose certain homes and relationships, so does the soul choose its habitats and relationships.

The soul's need to have specific physical energies from the Earth, in combination with certain family contacts and other human relationships, sets the initial scenario for the soul's drama called life. Your soul has free will choice selections before birth. This soul's choice is not generally understood by humans, however, until they acknowledge God and begin a connection to their own soul's guidance. That is why contemplation and meditation are so important! Through the soul's guidance your life can be enriched and fulfilling.

That blueprint which your soul made before incarnating into Earth had to be incorporated into a genetic coding compiled by the higher hosts of creation during the process of conception. This is done through the genetic coding of the DNA/RNA when the spiritual body interconnects, through the dynamics of the energetic fields (rays), to the physical body that is about to be birthed. With the soul's higher wisdom it will create the blueprint for the mental, emotional and physical body to experience while journeying through the Earth school for this particular life. As the soul enters the physical body amidst the kaleidoscope of color and sound, the baby's first breath activates the light body's blueprint that has previously selected which color and sound location it needs. Remarkably, the breath's pulsation is an automatic energy force that sets everything in motion and brings the soul's plan to Earth.

It is regrettable that most human ears cannot hear Earth's musical sounds and cannot see the glorious spectrum of indescribable colors that flow in and around her, their own bodies, and all living things. Each of the Earth's harmonic ley lines emit wondrous tones in a variety of hues that dance and sparkle, connecting your body to both the Cosmos and also to the inner world portals and the entrances within the Earth herself.

To help you appreciate some of this glorious color and

sound, I will now ask you to imagine ten intermingled colored rays pouring down from spiritual domains or angelic realms and surrounding the entire planet. See Earth bathed in this glorious light embrace of every color or ray you have ever seen. There are actually far more than ten colors or rays all glowing together, of course, but by selecting ten colors out of the myriad, we can provide a simple explanation that will be useful. Take a moment to envision this glorious colored light.

In ways your mathematics and physics have yet to verify, each ray's color translates into spiritual influences for those living within their color spectrum's influence. I want to emphasize that God geometrizes—and that mathematics is a universal language that can be expressed in light, sound and color. Even the letters of the alphabet have sounds that relate to numerical equivalents. Therefore, *names are essentially numbers.* Now from your vision of the beauty of those ten multi-colored rays surrounding the Earth, observe that some are being drawn down into certain places on Earth by mathematical connections to the vibration of their names. For example, New York State is drawing the color yellow.

These ten color rays are available to all humans, regardless of their physical location, race, gender, culture, age or religious beliefs. However, to demonstrate how one ray or color can be specifically drawn out from the entire color spectrum surrounding Earth and focused on a particular named area, I am presenting this Harmonic Chord Table to show you how the colors affect each state in the United States.

Please refer to **Table #1 on page 14** that contains information about the United States vortices and state colors and notice that each state has one of the ten colors as its own particular ray. Because there are 50 states, of course, the same color appears in more than one place. Remember that these grids with their color and sound influences do not compel, but offer supportive motivation to help the soul succeed with the lessons that it chose to be experienced. Since the soul is guiding you—its personality aspect—toward certain decisions and actions, your personal free will choices are crucial to the soul's plan. It is a delicate balance between your personality and your soul with the potential for growth and service hanging in the balance.

As you Americans look at the U.S. (Table #1, page 14) and find the state in which you were born, notice its color and then check the explanation that follows on page 63 for a brief description of the color's influence. As you evaluate the influences of your home state's color, you may or may not immediately see a direct connection with what you read. Just contemplate it without judgment. As there are no rights and wrongs to what you will notice, these brief comments are only a stepping stone for inner reflection.

If you do not see a relationship to the description of your birthplace's influence, ask yourself just what qualities you seemed to be acquiring from that particular region and ask for dreams and guidance to assist your understanding. You may wish to look through the other color influences as part of your contemplation. If you are willing to have an open attitude you will eventually gain insight. Sometimes a personality will live in only one location all its life. If so, that is the only grid activity that was necessary for it to encounter. However, for a variety of reasons most souls will have several or multiple moves throughout a lifetime.

For those of you who do not live in the United States, look at the place that you were born as a deliberate soulful choice and contemplate which color ray you feel might have influenced you on that grid. Since many of you have studied about chakras and color application to the body, remember that these ten colors I'm describing are the *grid* colors. Trained psychologists, teachers, counselors, astrologers, numerologists and psychics may have other interpretations based upon their prior training in other systems. Nonetheless, I invite an open mind and a sense of exploration as you read the simple introduction that I outline here.

GRID COLOR HARMONIC INFLUENCES

Red: Intellectual and Pioneering

The red grid's main influence is to expedite the inner power of one's will, through various situations that will call this forth. It stimulates the individual to be independent, sometime alone, courageous, ambitious, and generally to learn how to take charge of its own life.

Red vibration in balance: Creativity, assertiveness and originality, initiating, pioneering, developing inner will and strength.

Red vibration challenges: Dominating, being egotistic, headstrong, selfish, imitative and indecisive.

Orange: Teamwork and Intuition

The orange grid holds the law of cooperation, tact and diplomacy. Some individuals will have to learn to take back their power during this grid line's influence. The intuitive abilities are enhanced during this time through awakened sensitivity to circumstances beyond one's control. Partnership with oneself and connecting with others to work in a group effort is meaningful.

Orange vibration in balance: Diplomacy, sensitivity, patience, being secretive and quiet, being a peacemaker.

Orange vibration challenges: Over-sensitive, vacillating, being pessimistic, and cowardly.

Yellow: Communication and Creativity

The yellow grid will enhance the meaning of family life, social life, and connecting with people. Life on this grid can be your stage, and sometimes you may feel like a jack of all trades, learning to move easily and freely among people. This grid holds the power for ultimate language and communication ability in all fields of life—music, arts, theater, writing and lecturing.

Yellow vibration in balance: Self-expression, talent with words, imagination and optimism.

Yellow vibration challenges: Worrying, faultfinding,

self-admiration and extravagance.

Green: Builder and Worker

The green grid symbolizes a square, meaning that life itself will be rendering circumstances to learn self-discipline, routine, paying attention to details, being practical and demonstrating loyalty to work, family and country. This grid line will ask those under this vibration to maintain their balance and not shirk their responsibilities or duties. Logic is the tool to build, manage, and bring ideas into a manifested form.

Green vibration in balance: Diligence, being practical, untiring, and strong.

Green vibration challenges: Procrastinating, crude, being unprepared, idle, and stubborn.

Blue: Freedom and Change

The blue grid stimulates a mercurial nature of enthusiasm, energy, adventure, versatility and cleverness. Freedom of ideals, speech, and beliefs will be important to demonstrate and maintain. Under this grid one will want to discard the old and ineffectual, and embrace the new.

Blue vibration in balance: Analytical, open, inquiring, versatile, and understanding.

Blue vibration challenges: Being irresponsible, absurd, egocentric, inconsiderate, and erratic.

Indigo: Service and Teaching

The indigo grid initiates service and responsibility for the welfare of others. You will be given opportunities to work with family, social services and especially with people in groups. This grid assists in opening higher personal standards and ideals of life. You may be asked to serve the maladjusted and the ill, even though it may be difficult at times. This service will help you gain greater personal strength.

Indigo vibration in balance: Being loving, being artistic, healing, teaching, being responsible, and tolerant.

Indigo vibration challenges: Prying, interrupting, being self-righteous and reluctant to serve.

Lavender: Perfection and Idealism

The lavender grid initiates a focus on seeking perfection in developing mental powers to a highly evolved state of being and awakening, through deep levels of meditation or prayer, to the greater mysteries of life. This grid activates the intellectual abilities and interests toward the cultural, musical, mystical and philosophical.

Lavender vibration in balance: Mental, wisdom, silence, and spiritual peace.

Lavender vibration challenges: Being indifferent, baffled, nervous, and moody.

Burgundy: Leadership, System and Order

The burgundy grid will activate a life of study, organizational ability and executive powers. This grid will assist you in bringing strength, courage, poise and determination into your life. There will be a deep inner desire for power and control and a tendency to create success in material matters. This will usually enhance the desire to take charge and create a position of control and influence.

Burgundy vibration in balance: Power, material success, executive ability, control and leadership qualities.

Burgundy vibration challenges: Ambition for self, intolerance, and ruthlessness.

Pastels: Humanitarianism & Metaphysical Proficiency

The pastel grid holds a vibration of universal love and high aspirations to assist humanity. Love, generosity and perfection are the prime goals in your development. Great times of solitude, meditation and periods of silence are needed for this proficiency to develop. This energy focuses toward the search for universal truth and the use of these truths as an inspiration to others. Tolerance and understanding is the key of the pastel grid.

Pastel vibration in balance: Love of humanity, genius qualities, compassion, and forgiveness.

Pastel vibration challenges: Apathetic, self-important, vain, spiritually self-seeking, and prideful.

Silver: Creativity and Higher Intelligence

The silver grid catapults you into greater creativity and higher levels of thought that must be manifested into a physical form. This grid opens the psychic, artistic, philosophical and mystical desires of the soul. Many of the inventors, scientists, visionaries, and futurists are birthed into this grid line. The silver grid always initiates the new to be brought into expression and brings hope for a higher way of being and living.

Silver vibration in balance: Idealism, inventiveness, originality, humanitarianism, being a genius.

Silver vibration challenges: Narrow-mindedness, abuse of power, narcissism.

As you read these basic colors, please remember that each color has a multiplicity of hues and various expressions that assists your soul's evolution, depending on your willingness and consciousness level. I have clarified for you the influence that your soul had in planning this life as you deliberately incarnated onto a living planet expressing God's electro-magnetic patterns. This means you are intuitively aware that your physical location is very important in achieving the purposes of your soul. Consequently, you must recognize that your ultimate destination will be located among the appropriate Earth grids, vortices, and ley lines, which will support your highest evolution.

Of course, there are many healing, educational, and spiritual centers and communities already formed that take advantage of Earth's various energies. However, because there are many other regional power sites ready to be activated, I want to stress the unique opportunity for the star seeds, star children, and star lights to be influenced by both the celestial and inner worlds cities related to the Four Corners area in America.

I shall pause now and ask for your questions, Virginia.

* * *

VE: With gratitude we meet once again and I thank you for your informative sharing. Now let me begin some inquiries. For starters, how can the Archangel Gabriel transmute carbon into silicon or silica? We're beginning to realize how power-ful you archangels are, but changing a dense form into a different, more subtle element seems mind-boggling.

AM: He does this by utilizing particles of Sun/light to spin the Earth into a higher frequency. Silicon is less dense and is lighter than carbon so a gradual change is happening. Every planet or system can be rearranged by being re-positioned into a higher, more elevated frequency. So as Earth spins into a higher velocity rate, it cannot stay in the frequency of solid-ity. Consequently, linear time is accelerating into space-time. If you reflect about your busy life, you will notice time is ac-celerating and you never seem to have enough of it. It is the same for your human body today. As you consciously hold more positive thoughts you automatically elevate into a higher vibration. As you become filled with more light, you neutralize the lower frequency of darkness, and you will change from a physical body to a physical-etheric body. Everything solid is becoming lighter, beloved ones, by our ef-forts and yours. This is a simple explanation of the evolution of change.

VE: This is a pretty enormous event for the planet and us?

AM: Yes! Everything is in a pattern of change. It is inevi-table because everything on Earth is temporary. There is nothing permanent. All planets, star systems, and life forms throughout creation must change, because the eternal spiral of infinity uses involution to create evolution.

VE: I understand. We just have to trust that everything is in divine right order even if we can't always comprehend it fully.

AM: Do you not have to trust everything, through the act of faith, when it comes from the Father/Mother God? Every religious thought and practice today is being done on the basis of former writings, teachings and beliefs carried down through generations. For example, at this time of existence does the general population see Abraham, Moses, Buddha, Mohammed or Jesus and other great beings? No...and yet millions and millions of people pray, meditate and live their lives by trusting in what has been written or taught as truth by them. It is all blind faith.

VE: Agreed. Now I'd like to ask this question. How can the genetic coding of a person's physical life be controlled by a non-physical force like its soul? Some people may have a difficult time understanding this, especially if they were born blind, crippled, deaf, disfigured, and so forth. How should they react to this explanation that their physical difficulty is a deliberate choice?

AM: Through the journey of life, your soul has the freedom to choose what it wants to experience. As an example, if a soul chooses to be born physically blind, or is blinded during its life journey, the soul may have blinded another being in a previous life experience. Or the soul may want to experience blindness to obtain wisdom through the experience. Perhaps in one of its future lives it will be a doctor or a healer of the blind. In either case, the soul is choosing the experience to bring balance through the debt of karma or to gain spiritual growth and wisdom.

There is never judgment from God because it is pure love and knows nothing else. However, the soul will look upon the mirror of self and see where it yet needs to bring balance. This is called the law of action and reaction, or cause and effect. Every negative act that brings injury or harm to another will have to be experienced in some similar event to erase the karmic debt of imbalance—unless there is the intervening variable you call grace.

VE: Thank you. Now, referring to the list of the colors of the states being influenced by the ten harmonic chord frequencies—do the colors ever change? For instance, at a different historical period when the names were changed from the Louisiana Purchase; to the present day state of Louisiana, are the vibrations identical?

AM: No, it would hold a different frequency because the consciousness was different. In using the language of frequency, every name, name of a city, state or country, holds its own pattern of vibration containing a life force action frequency. For example, many people are changing their names during this time period. When a name is changed, it holds a blueprint of energy in order to fulfill a new purpose of destiny. In the Bible, Saul was given the new name Paul, which carried a different energy vibration that assisted him to fulfill an unsuspected destiny. Sometimes names are given by spirit, but people may also be personally motivated to change their own name. Others acquire new names through their professions or abilities, and many women change their purposes as they assume the last name of their marriage partner. Regardless, when the name is changed it holds a different pattern to assist in the accomplishment of purpose.

VE: Fine. The next question is this. Sometimes our soul is urging us to move someplace else but we choose to ignore it. Can you clarify how ignoring our soul's choice to live in a particular place might affect us?

AM: When the personality does not follow that particular direction, it is not time to move forward. Many think that they will never move, but then circumstances begin to come up, such as losing a job and not finding another one in that location. Events begin to occur that indicate the current home is no longer harmonious. Or the environment changes through floods, hurricanes, or earthquakes and you will find yourself being moved instantly. Your soul knows what you next need to experience, and at the appropriate time you will be there. Many of you leave because you feel very strongly within you that it is time, so you don't resist. You follow the guidance with ease, not always understanding why, but trusting it nevertheless. However, there are those who are more tenacious in wanting to maintain personal control, so the soul will set up situations for the personality to undergo in order to create a shift in consciousness. All of you come to crossroads in life and you must make a choice to go either left, right, or straight ahead. Each road will hold different experiences, but regardless of what road is chosen, it will still take you to the ultimate goal intended. Each of you has a soul plan that must be realized and fulfilled.

VE: So are you saying that even if we take a detour, we will still eventually get there?

AM: Yes, that is correct.

VE: I now have a question about the Central Sun, which you mentioned earlier in the book. Can you explain more about it for us?

AM: The energy from the Central Sun, which is the source called God, the Almighty, is the eternal expression of pure love. I, Archangel Michael, am from the Central Sun and have been asked to interpenetrate and to spread the blue flame ray to create a higher energy of light upon the Earth. This is causing your Earth to shift and uplift to a higher enlightenment. Remember it is the particles of the Sun/light that rearrange carbon into silicon/crystal. Simply put, God is calling for its own, and those who can absorb this energy will awaken, become God realized, unveil greater gifts of spirit, and work to help pave the way to a greater world of peace. If we stopped sending the light rays to Earth there would not be an ascension!

However, chaos can surface when an individual cannot tolerate the rays of light, and in this case many will have to look within and transmute the negative patterns that are creating havoc with their lives. But light will continue, and those who are ready, will be ready, and those who are not, will not. The power of the rays of the Central Sun is necessary to help you become enlightened and awakened, so we can bring everyone who acknowledges the Creator back home to the higher dimensions.

Chapter 5

The Tribunal Godhead & the Holographic Computer

Because you cannot see the Central Flame of Life called God, it is impossible to understand its essence, power and authority. But this description will attempt to give you a visionary image of what I call the Tribunal Godhead or the Divine Circle with a blue flame radiating from its center. The blue flame energy creates from within itself the symbol of the three Holy of Holies who are standing in a geometric design that formulates a triangle within a circle. One Holy of Holies is in the front with the other two in the back, one on the right side and the other on the left. These three Holies symbolize the eternal breath that resides in each soul, that infinite trinity that on Earth has been called Father/Mother God. You on Earth experience this trinity, or essence, through the Sun and the atomic particles, which are the proton, neutron and electron. The Central Flame of Life or Oneness has personified itself into three dynamic life forces through the geometrical symbol of the Divine Trinity.

The collected unity of those three aspects of God can be referred to as the brilliant flames of eternity who eventually created seven other flames that also directly connect to the

Flame of Life. These androgynous seven flames of spirit are the personification of the Divine that are known as the universal agencies or groups of one mind thought that were sent into the void, or the awaiting womb of potential creativity, necessary to begin the vast work that would follow. You may perceive this divine entry into the void as the birthing of all life—omniverses, universes, worlds within worlds, dimensions within dimensions. These seven flames have the power to create worlds for they hold the flame of Oneness.

After a time, the seven mystic flames also birthed forth twelve eternals who for the first time would have gender—masculine and feminine characteristics—and would go out beyond the blue flame of their central home to create spiritual, etheric and inter-dimensional worlds. Their essence began the seeding of the first genetic matrix and the spiral of everlasting life—eternity.

From the created worlds of the twelve eternals there was a later need for other beings of service and so they appointed executives to oversee these inner dimensions and the many angelic levels to overview the golden band of continuous thought or the everlasting breath.

Eons ago, when that part of your soul chose to leave the Source, you had the ability to bring forth many aspects of yourself by splitting yourself simultaneously into multi-dimensions at the same time. Though it may be difficult to believe, your original human soul is part of the great Flame of Life, which is the eternal breath that carries the life force energy needed to have simultaneous experiences throughout the many multi-dimensional levels.

For you on Earth, the symbolic representation of your numeric sequence of the three, the seven and the twelve essences of the Central Flame calculates for humans to the mystical/magical number of the 22. (3+7+12=22). For you, the 22 is an important number because it helps to raise you from the physical to the physical-etheric or the vibration of self-mastery and self-sovereignty.

The seed of your soul, from whence you have come, never leaves the central part of itself, but continues to procreate from within itself many multiple forms. *You have 144,000 dimensional aspects of yourself, all of which have split off from the soul's beginning nature and are simultaneously evolving throughout other worlds even now. Somewhere in time, all aspects will find each other and come back into original divineness. Then the soul seed will choose to re-create itself again into a grander degree of glory that awaits all the souls in their higher consciousness ascension.*

When you have ascended from one plane of existence, school or degree of soul growth, you enter into another dimension, only to prepare and learn to ascend again, and then again, and again—which is why it is called eternity or everlasting life. There is no end of existence, only the eternal breath re-creating itself through the various planes of existence and multiple forms forever.

All creations, dimensions, and worlds within worlds are assigned an executive or a universal agency that oversees your dominion and keeps the records or data on every living soul regarding its progress. You have called this the Akashic records, but in the higher Universe this is actually the Holographic Computer. There is not one thought, deed, or act that you do that is not accounted for and recorded in what we call the Holographic Computer.

This is a sophisticated device inscribing information about all life forms throughout the universes of creation. It is a marvel beyond your comprehension! Therefore, since few mortals are allowed to enter this awesome data center I would like to describe the experience that such a privileged mortal would have in entering the Holographic Computer. To give you an idea of what the mortal would experience, let me take you on an imaginary journey that must begin in the land of Egypt. We will go to the Egypt that you know today because there are invisible entry portals there.

THE HOLOGRAPHIC COMPUTER

Here between the feet of the Sphinx near the pyramid of Giza, there is a time portal that can energetically lead to Earth's Holographic Computer. However, it is necessary at this point for your subtle body fields to be raised to a compatible frequency using sound and light. Only if you are spiritually compatible will the celestial guardians activate the musical tones needed to increase the vibratory rate so the entrance will open. Through this process a spinning shaft of light will temporarily break the "force shield" and allow you to pass through it. Once admitted, you go down the spiral crystal staircase that holds the crystalline memory of the atomic rays (the elements of the Sun).

The use of the inverted position of the pyramid opens a portal to enter the vibratory dimensional realm. Then you can pass through this portal into one of the rainbow cities of Earth that hold different energy vibrations. These cities have councils who encircle and telepathically greet the visitor using the ancient greeting, "Timo, Timo," which means everyone recognizes you have come with the Divine Council of Honor. These beings are dressed in white robes, and a golden aura crowns the top of their heads. What appears to the mind's eye as golden sandals upon their feet, are actually energetic flotation pads that can be used to rapidly exit and enter into various other dimensions.

If you could enter into such a city you might well be surrounded in a circle of light created by those who can use their minds in unison. In front of you there would be a vortex of light containing a large crystalline cube with a blue flame rising out of its center. Since this is not a consuming flame of fire but an eternal flame, when you enter it the vibration increases and you can be teleported by the "orbital evaluator."

The orbital evaluator is a faceted fire crystal that contains the power of the Sun for creating a teleportation route. This orbital evaluator is a higher mathematical device connecting with the inter-dimensional ley lines that contain light, color, and sound. It is these frequencies that now assist in taking the physical-etheric bodies instantaneously into another dimension.

Please try to imagine that you have been teleported to a circular room where the dynamics of light are far greater than anything that you have ever seen through your physical sight while on Earth. In unending vistas you can see a crystal city whose architectural design is based upon the geometrical configurations of circles within circles, triangles within triangles, cubes within cubes. Within the angles of each design a vibratory rate is produced. Now you can look into the center of this fabulous city, which you realize, is the Holographic Computer.

The Holographic Computer is immense because it contains within it the collective essence of this planet, which is connected to the Universe. This holographic mainframe connects to a central matrix, which in turn connects to all the planetary, galactic, and solar system programs that activate all the invisible grids. These programs hold many of the various harmonic chord formulas that create the inter-stellar mapping systems of grids, spider web formations, ley lines, and routes through space.

There are many frequency programs that have multiple levels of programmed thought banks containing knowledge of a scientific, mathematical, and aeronautical nature. There are also many musical scores and varied recorded data within the grid codes.

These programs are coded frequencies that bring forth the variances of the universal language throughout the many realms, dimensions, and planes of existence in the Universe. Universal language is different than the telepathic mind level and its state of evolution. While you may tend to think of the Holographic Computer like a computer in your own world, I assure you that your computers are extremely primitive in their use of transmitted and received knowledge.

The Holographic Computer can translate telepathic

thought throughout all dimensions and universes. There are celestial beings who record data through the Holographic Computer moment by moment. Every soul who has ever been birthed is recorded within the mainframe through the dynamics of what you understand as a genetic coding. However, the genetic coding is enormously expansive and goes beyond the genetics of the human species. As you are learning, there are innumerable physical forms who reside in many of the heavenly realms, and they are different from your own earthly body. Nonetheless, the Holographic Computer has stored data on every frequency of each soul—its deeds, actions, thoughts, location, and movements.

Let us pause a moment now because there is something vital that I wish to take time to describe—something that may be a new perception for you to entertain. You see, your own soul can experience itself by recreating multi-faceted forms that are placed throughout the Universe so these forms can simultaneously interface with one another. In this way the experiences of both individuals and groups are known and recorded as a collective species for evolutionary advancement.

This is done by creating multiple levels of helix strands of genetic coding. You—the souls on Earth—are connected to the double helix and are awakening to uplift to the triple helix and the quadruple helix. Eventually there will be vibratory frequencies of body and soul called the pentad, hexad, heptad, ogdoad, and ennead helixes as future embodiments throughout the higher realms of created forms. Of course, there are innumerable other species with different elementary cellular patterns.

Your own DNA contains life essences that hold physical and subtle body knowledge about the past, present and future of the whole spiritual creation. The RNA, within the brain terminal of each body, carries cell memories that are used to activate the whole genetic coding within each being. The original genetic coding and its pattern are designed by the Creator for specific soul purposes. After the soul evaluates its life experience and is ready to be re-created into another bodily form, the celestial helpers activate the new genetic patterns created for that life purpose. They then activate the current genetic code by connecting or attaching the code to various light rays of the soul's energy field. The coding blueprint for the learning to begin in the next incarnation has now been set in motion.

Just as I described that there is a Holographic Computer that we placed within the center of your planet when Earth was created, so every planet, star system and universe has its own Holographic Computer. These computers can instantaneously be activated to include all systems or a single system. However, the Holographic Computer is never actually totally activated until life begins. In this way the higher realms can monitor and overview all the species of Earth, for example, and follow their development. Although many people believe the center of Earth is only solid, gaseous, or volcanic, there are invisible portals that can be entered by celestials for evolutionary support. Your Holographic Computer on Earth is programming, recording, and dispersing data back to the main frame to be stored and sealed until the information is opened to begin again at the various levels of ascension.

It is urgent that you understand that there will come a moment on your Earth when God's voice will be heard simultaneously by every single human regardless of their country, gender, religion, or language. That message will be: "THE TIME IS NOW! FOR I HAVE SPOKEN." The Earth will rumble, the curtains of heaven will open, and everyone throughout the whole of the Universe, including humanity, will hear the voice of Oneness. Upon hearing God's message, I will gather all the Legions of Light and I will uplift all beings according to their high vibratory field of light so these can proceed to begin another world.

You might wonder how everyone could simultaneously hear the word of God. It is because God's energy activates the holographic mainframe throughout all the central matrices into all the interconnected computers. As they connect together, the multi-levels of intricate sounds will create a kaleidoscope of telepathic language that will translate into a voice that can be heard by every soul upon the Earth and all through the heavens. This is truly what is known as "the ascension."

When the announced ascension occurs no one needs to go to a mountain or to some sacred place. Everyone will be in their correct location wherever they are at this awesome moment and will be identified by the frequency level of their soul field.

Please contemplate that while your everyday life is serious preparation for an eventual spiritual graduation or possible ascension, the higher dominions and I want you to appreciate your *daily* life. Using positive thought every day has never been more important to you in experiencing beauty, joy and caring for yourself, other people, and all life on the planet.

This book is called Earth, the Cosmos and You because we want you to expand and express your own inner kingdom in order to have fuller awareness of both your glorious planet and all that lies beyond in the Cosmos.

This inner kingdom of yours, about which we so often speak, is actually the source of light, which we call the Flower of Fire or the power of the Central Sun. The more often you intimately connect with this Flower of Fire within your own essence, the more you can travel among the corridors of your true origins. Because this is so important for your joy and self-realization I want to offer a simple practice to assist you in traveling the inner dimensions leading to your own soul's energy.

This practice begins with a short statement of intention such as "I am now ready and prepared to begin this medita-tion." (If you have another similar statement or spiritual ritual use it. You may also mention the name of an angel or master if that feels appropriate. Use whatever is comfortable.)

Visualize or think of two colors—bright red and indigo blue, which will immediately blend into the vibration of magenta or a rich ruby hue. Simultaneously say or tone, either aloud or silently, FA, RE, TI, (the musical notes F, D, and B.) This combination of colors and sounds opens a doorway to your own Flower of Fire which interlaces with your own soul, located behind the physical heart.

I suggest you feel or imagine this wondrous ruby Flower of Fire and the accompanying tones FA, RE, TI, whenever you need protection, support or encouragement, or to transmute negativity. This process only takes a minute once you have mastered the technique and is very useful for maintaining balance and stability during disruptions or challenging experiences. By practicing this process consistently it can activate your Flower of Fire so it can open its energetic fields which are connected to the Holographic Computer. This can begin to unveil the cell memories of your latent gifts and spiritual knowledge more consciously. This process will strengthen your telepathic ability to communicate with beings of light within Earth's Inner Worlds and the celestial or cosmic dimensions as well.

Now then, Virginia, what questions do you have for me today?

* * *

VE: Greetings to you once again. We are most grateful for your revealing comments. Because the news regarding each soul having 144,000 aspects of itself is something I hadn't known before, can you say more about that?

AM: The seed of the soul always remains in the center of the living Oneness or the Source. As I have already mentioned, in the beginning the Source birthed souls from within its eternal nature. Therefore, the soul has the ability to recreate itself in multiples of 144,000 (1+4+4=9) x 144,000 and on and on—so it is never ending. It is humanly impossible for you to comprehend the act of creation, but by using the dynamics of the sacred number 144,000, you may come to better appreciate the magnificence of your soul heritage. *You have many counterparts or fractionalizations of yourself that co-exist* *with you through the multiples of worlds within worlds.*

Try to comprehend that because Oneness births souls from within itself they are its expression, and since Oneness itself is eternal, so is the soul! In your present dimension it is difficult to comprehend the glory of this but it means you will be loved forever! And through your intrinsic nature, you will be able to love whenever you choose it. I used this number 144,000 because it is sacred, it holds the vibration of universal love, and it means completion with the choice to begin again.

VE: So there must be a gargantuan number of souls out there. Does anyone know how many?

AM: Oh beloved soul, how many creations are there? The number couldn't even register within your mathematical calculations. Just understand that it is as countless as eternity. That is why I used the geometrical sacred number of 144,000 as the language of the Universe to assist you in understanding that life is always expanding, completing, only to begin again. *Life is forever!*

VE: That's thrilling! I love to be reminded. Now here is a question we struggle to understand. We have on our planet this big argument between Darwinism, which is our evolution from lower species, versus Creationism, that says God created man. Can you explain this and the close genetic relationship between animals, apes, and humans?

AM: There are multiples of Genesis and all species have their own genetic coding inlaid for the embodiment they need for their experiences. What mankind doesn't understand is that life has always been, and by the process of involution to evolution souls choose to take various forms to grow. I know that many will disagree with the concept that animals, vegetation, etc., are also soul enmeshed. But let me ask you, what is soul?

In the higher equations, soul is the root base equal to form. Every life form has the living breath of God within it, whether mineral, vegetable, animal or human. There is nothing that exists on Earth, in the Universe, or Omniverse that is not created by and through the living essence of the Source. So are you not all inter-related through the process of breath? There are many forms far beyond your comprehension or imagination. Throughout the higher worlds, inner worlds, and celestial planes there are forms that would appear to be animal-like, or even grotesque to you. However, it is simply another form that the soul created to function within the particular vibrational pattern that a specific system holds in order to experience life. Everything has a genetic coding, and genetics is the life path of creation. The genetics that you know through the source of life that exists on your Earth isn't the totality of creation!

Whether you have come from the natural process (holding the genetic patterns within the same species) or through the doors of genetically being created by the higher creative forces, you are still a part of the Oneness. You are all inter-laced within the webbing of creation as one life. Actually, both explanations of evolution hold some rightness, but I would ask you to observe that all life is from the divine plane of Oneness. You inter-relate as brothers and sisters regardless of form.

I say this kindly. You will never be able to truly understand evolution while you are in a three-dimensional realm. Even others in the multiple worlds do not understand its totality. You can have theory upon theory but it would be impossible for you to comprehend. It is one of the mysteries of life that your scientists are still trying to solve—and that's just for the species called human. Try to grasp that there are many Adams and many Eves meaning Atom and the Evolutionary process. If you truly understood the concept of creation, and the nature of the source you call God, religion would no longer be practiced as it is in your world. (It would be far different just as it is in the celestial kingdoms.)

VE: You spoke earlier about the human species having the double helix and awakening to the triple helix. There are some people who presume that this is going to be happening very quickly. Could you clarify the time line regarding this

DNA advancement?

AM: I know many people do think that they already have their fourth or even their twelfth helix strand, but if that were so, they would no longer reside upon this planet. Many humans are working to attain a higher vibration, but this will only take place as the souls release negativity and awaken to the higher states of being. Each soul will move into the additional DNA strands of life by accelerating through the doorways of ascension. You cannot hold the higher helix strands and stay physically dense. Thus you must become a physical-etheric being and elevate to a higher state of light.

VE: Are any of those 144,000 soul aspects you've described ever with us in our current lifetime?

AM: Let me answer by using some familiar terms you've developed such as soul mates, twin souls and walk-ins. Our definition of a soul mate is when two intimate individuals—often marriage partners—come back together for a life of spiritual completion and a strong service contribution. A twin soul is the supportive vibration of a higher immortal, non-physical being, whose energy is shared with a mortal physical person living on the planet. A walk-in is an exchange when a higher counterpart of the soul takes over its current physical Earth body and personality to strengthen the success of its life purpose. This exchange can only happen during the physical body's unconscious state and must have mutual agreement of both parties.

Today, with the upcoming Earth changes and the promise of ascension, there are more of those walk-ins—or what we prefer to call "soul exchanges"—happening. This exchange avoids the long years of infancy and permits the strongest soul aspect its access to an adult body. This saves valuable time and can usually provide a greater contribution to the light. Soul exchanges must be pre-arranged and are not a thoughtless contract.

VE: Does any of this relate to what we call the "near death" experience?

AM: No, because a near death experience is a temporary out-of-body shift when the consciousness exits into a holding station in the astral world, usually caused by serious illness or a sudden accident. If its time on Earth is not complete the human is then returned to the everyday consciousness of its Earth life—usually with greater respect for God, life, and its spiritual purpose. Although your scientists disavow these experiences I can assure you they are real and can have enormous influence on those who undergo even this brief energy exposure in the doorway to heaven.

And now I want to tell you more about the many beings and regions that are presently influencing both your planet and humanity's consciousness.

EARTH, THE COSMOS AND YOU

Chapter 6

The Planetary Systems and Maldek

As humans look up into your mysterious night sky—your heavens—you cannot see the true gamut of incredible life that exists out there. This is because you are still within the confines of your three-dimensional illusions. However, your recent explorations into space are beginning to dissolve some of the illusion that you are physically alone in the solar system and galaxy. A primary lingering misconception you must release is that just as your Earth is a living being with both physical and spiritual energy fields, so every other planet is also a living creation, a microcosm of matter and spirit. So it's true that planets are physical, but also remember that they vibrate to the different frequencies of the four elements and are consequently very unique in size and structure.

Although you might be able to physically stand on another planet, such as Mars, you may not see any form of life, even though there are *underground* cities beneath the surface that hold a higher vibratory frequency! Through your explorations into space you may well see *above-ground* buildings, monolithic structures and pyramids, but until someone can hold a higher vibratory frequency while observing other planets the whole reality of their life will elude you.

It is because of your dense three-dimensional conscious-ness that you are baffled and confused about God and the many levels of creations beyond Earth. If you could even un-derstand what higher spiritual beings have already encoded in your holy books, some of the mystery would clear.

For example, many inspired authors of your biblical litera-ture recorded comments describing many celestial beings and how they came to Earth. Consider the true meaning of the statement, "In my Father's house are many mansions." This means that all the millions of star systems, galaxies, and plan-ets that are in your Universe are the celestial heavens and dimensions of "the Father"—or as Jesus actually said, "In my *Father/Mother's house* there are many mansions."

I want you to embrace the idea that your word "angel" has many, many meanings, and that there is great confusion about angels on planet Earth. This is because of the different vibratory frequencies celestial beings hold and the dimen-sions from whence they come. There are many angels from the higher stations of the Universe—the spiritual and soulic realms—that do not hold a physical form, but emanate a light energy field that is in service to both the higher and lower dominions. Some of these great angels who have never had human form, and seldom visit Earth, are confused with lower dimensional physical-etheric beings who are merely on the next higher spiritual level from humanity. (Some of these are described biblically as appearing in human form to Abraham and Lot and even eating a meal.)

The angels who are sent to assist humanity are the ap-pointed messengers of enlightenment, support, healing, encouragement, and protection. They are coming into the Earth now more than ever to assist with this Divine Interven-tion in preparation for the coming ascension. They come from many realms. This leads to enormous misunderstandings. Please understand that any non-terrestrial being who is com-municating can only be perceived or experienced at the spiritual awareness level of the humans with whom they come in contact—either through telepathy, voice, vision, or actual physical appearance.

Some of you on Earth have experienced an angel or the presence of one who has come to deliver messages of peace, announce changes, or offer prophetic information. There are also the angels who give guidance, encouragement, and protection, and who are your guardians as you travel through this life. There has recently been a great interest in angels because more of them are making their appearance to you on Earth so that you can awaken to this heavenly group of servants and higher degrees of life. In particular, Mother Mary apparitions and messages are more frequently being seen throughout your planet.

Because the higher realms and the angelic beings are so numerous within your Universe, and humanity cannot really comprehend the vastness of its expanses, I now wish to describe something about the technical and non-technical activities that the many different species and beings who work with Earth today have as their functions and services.

Positioned in your Universe there is a Central Sun that is a particle of the greater Sun from the Central Flame. Within this particle of light reside many of the more elevated Holy of Holies. For the benefit of the physical worlds, they appoint the executives to the positions within the physical-etheric realms, called the Intergalactic Federation. These semi-physical beings and systems are more advanced than humans and have highly technical specialty assignments such as fleet commanders, directors of space communications, celestial patrols, spaceship technicians, scientists, mathematicians, architects, pyramidologists, and guardians of the portals. Some of them are what you call UFO's and aliens.

On another less technical level there are those who educate and work in the various temples of enlightenment, and there are philosophers, physicians, musicians and artists, record keepers, scribes, keepers of cosmic law, accelerators of mental telepathy, space psychologists, and many others. I mention these activities because some of you reading this material have formerly had knowledge and experience with higher worlds and may feel a sense of familiarity with them. Many humans are awakening today and unveiling past memories in preparation for the new times ahead.

In order to trigger certain frequencies within you, and further expand some personal perceptions, let me share this information about some of the cosmic beings and regions who are particularly helping you and Earth ascend now. Over time, the civilizations on certain planets and star systems have tended to develop and advance in particular interests and specialties. Here are some examples.

THE GLOBAL COMMUNICATORS OF SATURN

The Saturnians are particularly known as Global Communicators because the rings of their planet emit beautiful harmonic chords or sounds that can be heard throughout the Universe. They connect with innumerable other systems. These Saturnian rings you have now seen in space are in reality clusters of fire crystals interlaced with intricate coils that have been placed in a spherical ring that emit symmetrical tones. Inside the planet itself there are huge sections that hold large colonnades or pillars of crystals and alloys that are tilted from 15° to 90° angles. Each pillar must be activated by the telepathic power of the Global Communicators using an energy pulsation called Ken-Levo. The Global Communicators must telepathically activate the proper mathematical formulas in sequential timing in order to communicate to any other particular planet or system.

When the pillars are activated they create a vibration pattern that emits sounds throughout the rings of Saturn. These colonnades or pillars can be programmed for transmitting and receiving information and are also used for grid travel routes. The Saturnians also have the capability to project holograms of information that connect to the higher councils for news—vaguely like your satellites, TV and radio stations.

Saturn is where one of the Supreme Councils resides, and from here they monitor all stellar activities in the Universe. Saturn is known as a central station for transferring communication with many other intelligence beings. Most Saturnians serve in the fields of communication and in space as controllers of the grid fields or travel routes through space. What is of special application to humanity is that the Saturnians are sending to many of you, and to other systems, a telepathic message using what is called the digital dot language. This system emits impulses that are heard in the inner ear as a high frequency pitch that sounds like a series of tones—similar to the SOS frequency. When this telepathic communication occurs you are receiving transmissions of information that will either be understood by you at the instant of the transmission, or released at a later time when it is appropriate. This is *not* the condition of the ear you call tinnitus. The Saturnians are important in monitoring the developmental process of your evolution and are closely observing what Earth and her inhabitants are choosing to do.

THE ANGELIC PHYSICIANS OF VENUS

Venus was once known as the planet called both Hesperus and Veda. It is a place of celestial beings who offer services of hope, healing and love. The angelic physicians can read the auric/soul fields of a human energy to help them understand what level of guidance the person still needs in order to transcend their own limitations and go through the next heavenly portal to a more elevated domain. Many of the angelic physicians are sent from Venus to assist those of you on Earth. More of you are seeing angels who appear during a crisis of sickness, and many humans are being healed. Whenever a human is experiencing a surgery, its light body is vulnerable because the anesthetic causes it to separate from the physical body. At this instant the angelic physicians come to maintain and assist in the protecting and healing of the etheric body while the medical doctors of Earth are attending to the physical body itself.

These angelic physicians are in service to assist in giving you direction, inspiration, protection and healing on all three levels of your physical, emotional and mental bodies. These Venusians also work together so you will be escorted to the various temples of healing during your sleep and dream time. Some humans want to quickly improve the level of healing just by using new technical energy devices. Others prefer the natural ways of healing using methods like herbs and organic resources of Mother Earth. As you open to your higher abilities you will discover that there are far greater tools for healing to be used on your planet than you have remembered thus far.

The Venusians are helping you to unveil these memories so that you can assist in the healing of many people during these times of change. However, it is essential to learn to use the power of your own mind and to connect with the center of your Source to heal yourself. The Venusians especially want to assist humanity in using their own God-given abilities to release the many addictions caused by the reliance on inappropriate or toxic drugs, and the overuse of some pharmaceutical products.

It is possible you will be utilizing even more of the higher techniques of healing now that you have the computer and light microscopes for detecting the vibrational fields of the blood and subtle bodies.

Those of you who have primarily been healers—from Venus or elsewhere in the Cosmos, or during the time of Lemuria—are now awakening to use your higher abilities in the healing processes. For those of you who feel that you hold greater levels of healing abilities within you and sincerely want to practice these spiritual talents, you can call upon the Venusians, and others, to assist in the opening of these talents. Nonetheless, there is an appropriate time for the awakening within each person that must be honored. Until then you all are being directed and given both the inspiration and the ability to heal yourself and to share your ever-increasing purity with those who ask for your assistance.

Always remember the greatest healing is taking place within yourselves.

The Venusians will be bringing both physical-etheric and physical rejuvenation chambers to Earth, so you will be able to rejuvenate all parts of your body, and also rearrange your genetic coding using the elements of the electro-magnetic fields of energy. These circular chambers will be built with the ᶜodes of geometrical energy patterns that will produce a vibrational frequency connecting with the lunar and solar ambient factors.

Many of you will experience health changes by visiting certain geographical places that hold dimensional pulses and can assist in the molecular and cellular rearrangement of physical forms. These "integration chambers" or structures will connect to all the grids and ley lines of your world. We know that on Earth you are presently doing your best to heal through drugs, herbs, electronics, mental imagery and surgery, but this will eventually be done more efficiently by the integrated energy chambers, a process presently being experimented with by a few Earth scientists.

The Venusians will also support you in teaching, nurturing and loving the animal kingdoms. They have many who are the teachers of these animals and who help them to evolve and get ready for their next existence. These animals also choose their Earth families in order to complete the ties of karma. For example, consider your pets called dogs. Dogs are among the most loyal of animals, and want to show their true nature, which was given by the Creator.

All animals are the creation of God, and they are sent to humanity for many purposes. Those who awaken to their God-self will respect animals, seeing the reflection of God in them. Many of you on Earth who are working so diligently to save the animals from the cruelties of man's lower nature, may have been those who experienced the planet Venus in physical-etheric form. There, you may have loved, taught, and supported these beings in the animal paradises. Now you may have come back again to awaken the collective consciousness through your dedication, devotion and demonstration of compassion and love for these wonderful animal beings.

THE MATRIARCHS OF CLARION

Clarion is a matriarchal system within this Universe that teaches the essential values of the feminine nature and gives guidance to many of the women and some men on your planet, as well as to those on other star systems. These Clarions prefer to hold physical-etheric forms that express more of the feminine nature than the masculine, just as certain angels appear as feminine or masculine, depending on what they have selected to emphasize within their vibrational field. These matriarchs have extraordinarily high telepathic powers and can also utilize the grids for inter-dimensional space travel on their journeys to raise the consciousness of all genders. Although strongly feminine, the Clarions also build and pilot their own wheels of mechanization (ships) and are preparing for the time when God's ascension word is spoken. They will join with the other Legions of Light to assist the planet Earth when she takes another position in the solar system.

Then you might think of Clarion as the "Cosmic Mother System," and many of your Earth women who are now responsibly taking charge of their own lives may either be former feminine beings from that planet or may currently be receiving their influence if requested. Earth women today are holding more positions of power and authority and are taking leadership positions to assist in the natural shift from a predominantly patriarchal to a more matriarchal societal system. You are having to awaken to your own self-realization, self-love, and to claim your power by employing certain masculine attributes within yourself. Women must hold firm to the quiet power of their strength, however, which is far greater than the physical strength of the masculine nature. Men, on the other hand, have to develop and express their inner feminine power in order to bring the necessary balance within themselves.

Remember, then, that Clarion is one of the planets of good will and divine love, and her matriarchs are advising all women to express their creative nature so that they can lead and inspire many people in these great times of change.

THE PYRAMIDOLOGISTS OF EPSILON BÖÖTES

Böötes is a star system that overviews and activates all pyramids throughout your Universe. You see, there are pyramids on and within each planet just as the physical-etheric beings built your pyramids upon the Earth long ago when they lived in Lemuria, Atlantis, and other civilizations. These pyramids were constructed for multiple reasons and purposes. They are energetically connected through the grid ley lines to activate the landing stations for inter-dimensional travel. They are also communication centers that hold recorded data and act as calendars of time and gateways to the inner dimensions.

They also store electro-magnetic fields of energy that can be used to heal and preserve many substances. (You on Earth are already using small pyramid models that serve your personal needs in this way. As a caution, for most people, I do not recommend sitting or sleeping under large metal pyramids because they connect and activate your subtle body fields at a very enhanced acceleration of frequency. When you use a pyramid it produces a temporary cellular elevation that unlocks suppressed memories and takes you into other states of being, which may not always be in your best interest.)

The beings of Böötes are the mathematicians who service the pyramids by means of their telepathic capabilities, using the geometrical symbols that can keep certain portals open and close others that are not usable at this time. These pyramidologists utilize the higher mathematics to design the individualized blueprints of pyramids that will be compatible with each planet's unique frequency. Certain humans who specialize in fields related to mathematics, engineering, and architectural design may be in connection with these beings on Böötes.

THE INNER WORLD GUARDIANS OF KNUPLIES

The Knuplians (nu-pleans) are not located in your particular solar system or galaxy, but are in your local Universe. They have many different positions universally but have the specific assignment to guard the inner world portals from harm and inappropriate entrance. They also guard the *ascension flames* situated throughout all systems of life. The ascension flame is a beautiful violet color interlaced with the transmutable blue flame of the Central Sun that creates a higher element of conducted energy not yet known on Earth. This flame is placed within each planet's orbital gateway in order to prevent the inhabitants from exiting their world or entering into another world until the time is correct for them to ascend into a graduated state.

For those of you who are feeling called to visit certain sacred sites and vortices, either individually or with a group, this would be an indicator that you are familiar with the ability to protect these portals, and also how to exit and enter into these various realms of existence. As you have experienced, group visits to such places can be powerful indeed. But you may only enter the portal with the approval of the Guardians of Knuplies.

MASTERS OF THE HARMONIC BOARDS OF ANSTREAM

Those who reside within the star system of Anstream are masters of celestial sound and so they teach ways of creating the greater harmonics of music throughout the many systems of the Universe. Their thoughts emit a frequency that projects various rays of color and tone, and these tones create a kaleidoscope of harmonic chords. They are the ones, through their telepathic voices in unison, who create the heavenly musical scores of symphonies within symphonies for all the heavens to hear. These Anstreameans also pave the way for others to utilize their tones or arrangements of musical melodies in order to accelerate into higher levels of dimensional experiences during their meditative contemplation.

Many of you on Earth who are playing music and learning tones through various instruments are being inspired by these beings on Anstream. They are sending you telepathic sounds within your mind so that you can write the various compositions from the higher spheres that help to uplift the hearts of humanity. The tones that are heard either by individuals, or by groups, can move you into the richer depths of your soul, which opens the Flower of Fire and helps you to awaken and unveil a necessary part of yourselves through the emotional body.

When the musicians on Earth hear these tones via their inner ear it is often the angelic choir that is transmitting this musical score for them to receive and then gift to humanity. So if you are writing, directing, singing, or playing the musical tones of this celestial level, you are probably assisting those on Earth to elevate to this higher language of the Cosmos. Tone is one of the components of the universal language that awakens the spirit within all life and removes the barriers and blocks held within the physical, emotional and mental bodies. More and more of you are also awakening to the use of these tones through your vocal chords as you sing, tone, and chant to heal, nurture, and bring hope and balance to humankind. If ever you are sad or ill, music can quickly raise your vibration in very profound ways, whether you sing yourself or listen to sounds that delight you. In ways difficult to describe, all of heaven sings and its song reminds you of your true essence.

YOUR UNIVERSAL OVERSEERS OF ARCTURUS

Arcturus is a powerful energy for Earth and humanity. It is connected to another system called Mazzaroth that is positioned in your local galaxy and is the dwelling place of the executive hierarchy who oversee your particular solar system and also influence other parts of the Universe. Arcturians are highly evolved spiritual beings who hold that creative power of the Universe for Earth. They are also essential to your transmission and reception of data from the Earth's

Holographic Computer. These valued celestials are monitoring and guiding the inhabitants of Earth to assure the future ascension of your Earth as well as the whole Universe. The Arcturians have always been essential to your development and will increasingly be important to you in your upcoming physical-etheric lives.

THE TIME PHILOSOPHERS OF ANDROMEDA

The Andromedans are the brother and sisterhood of what we term the Amethystine Order. They are the heavenly philosophers of creative expanded thought. They give birth to vital doctrines and concepts that will be opened and released at the appropriate time intervals throughout the systems of your Universe. These telepathic beings work in unison, and independently, to gather and produce what may be called "time-released" information. They have an ability to seal these doctrines of inspired thought into precious alloys of gold, silver and tolitium. This seal will be decoded at a particular moment of time in order for the knowledge to be used to advance the species and planet into a higher evolutionary state.

If the Andromedans seal their information collectively, as a group, then only a collective or group can open it at a later time. If it is sealed independently, it can only be decoded by a being who holds the same frequency. (You have many things on Earth you physically lock up and need a key or combination to open it again, which is a similar principle to sealing thoughts.) The Andromedans use their telepathic minds to seal the information by positioning the knowledge into a fire crystal orb, which is then dissected into different geometrical designs and placed into a tablet of alloy and sealed. These separate geometrical pieces hold the encoded formula in a time-release state that can only be opened by the beings themselves at a later date. Or they can transmit their sealed code information to another entity who can be the one to decode and deliver the news.

Throughout various periods of time, many writers and

philosophers have been given information to help change the consciousness within your planet. You may be one of those now awakening on the Earth plane who is experiencing an inner knowing that is vigorously motivating you to write and share your particular knowledge or expertise.

Indeed, some of you are those beings who resided within the Andromedan civilization who had encoded certain knowledge to be decoded and released at this moment of time on Earth. You knew, then, that this information would blend together with pieces held by others. You knew that the collective compilation of this information would assist humanity's evolution by releasing the necessary encoded information to create change.

Please realize I have only mentioned eight of the many important planets and star systems serving humanity and Earth today. These eight I have already mentioned are quite active helpmates along with the Pleiades, Polaris, Sirius, Vega and others about whom much has been written.

There are those of you on Earth who are awakening to the realization that you are not from the Earth plane, but that you have cosmic roots from various systems among the stars who are diligently working with you. Some of you focus primarily on an association with a single cosmic influence while others hold several or multiple cosmic relationships.

The important thing to remember is simply this. Your past powers have been planned and coordinated to intersect with this historical moment. What determines the outcome of the plan depends on your ability to stay conscious while living in a dense free-will dimension full of challenges and potential detours.

I hope this brief description of eight positive planetary groups who help you and Earth has brought you a feeling of gratitude and a sense of well being. At this time, however, it is important to understand that there have been inhabitants on some planets who have destroyed life by their misuse of powerful technological secrets and weapons. Since one such planet was nearby in your own solar system, I must speak frankly about it and clarify how the past events there are affecting your own planet even as I speak. Some of you may have already heard about the plant Maldek but I shall present the basic facts so we may have a common understanding.

THE WAYWARD PLANET OF MALDEK

Although you may not see a connection between the present asteroid belt in your solar system and a former planet called Maldek, which was destroyed, I need to explain this connection because it relates to the settlement of planet Earth.

The Maldekian's were a superior physical-etheric race who were connected with many of the planetary systems by their telepathic abilities, knowledge and desire to maintain a law of oneness. They had many beautiful institutes of learning and used a point system of graduated rewards and service credits leading to continuous growth rather than a monetary reward system. Their lives were similar but superior to the later civilizations begun in Lemuria, Atlantis, and early Egypt.

The beings on Maldek originally vibrated as a higher form of life until Lucifer began to drop negative thoughts into the minds of many who were willing to receive them. The non-human Maldekians were highly telepathic and could instantly manifest many things according to each of their talents and specialties. Their major objective on Maldek was to telepathically broadcast to other beings in the systems of your Universe in order to share vital information necessary to maintain planetary safety and well being. Some of the planets with which they communicated were allies, and when compatible alliances were established they would connect their sub-stations to exchange certain formulas, calculations and higher technology related to their crystal civilizations. Some of the information related to fire crystals called double-pointed energy rods. These rods were originally installed to stabilize and maintain planetary balance. **(See Illustration # 12, next page)**

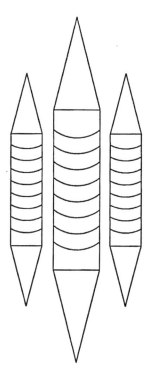

Illustration # 12 - Double-pointed Energy Rods

These huge fire crystal energy rods stood like vertical towers of enormous height. They contained special formulas for scientific projects, space data, and travelling formulas for entering and exiting many dimensions. These energy rods were also connected to the Holographic Computer and held genetic keys for recording the evolutionary growth of various species throughout the planetary systems. The energy rods issued an alert to ward off attacks of misguided meteors and to protect atmospheric conditions.

As time passed, unrest began and there were those who wanted to take control over both Maldek's citizens and over other planets as well. The long established council of judicious wisdom was replaced by a new council of initiators who gained power over the people and no longer allowed freedom of choice. The new regime began to install monitoring systems which they placed in homes, work stations, foundations of learning, library systems, and even the orbital systems of global communication.

The monitoring systems could record the thoughts and actions of everyone and identify those independent thinkers who disagreed with the thought controllers. Eventually implanted chips were placed inside the bodies of every citizen—and also at the front or back of the head. When citizens held thoughts against the government policies, the chips could be activated and actually immobilize the body. As the unrest grew stronger, greater controls were initiated and the misuse of atomic energy began moving the planet to its demise.

Finally, the other planets gathered together and unanimously agreed to dismantle the grid connectors which meant that the Maldekians were left on their own. They were told they would only be reconnected if they came back into thoughts of harmony. However, the leaders still chose to continue misusing the fire crystal rays and placed even more restrictive rules on its people.

Because many of the Maldekians did not agree with what the council was implementing, they began to leave their planet before the final closure was put into effect. Of course those who left Maldek had to travel to the other inhabited planets to reside while Maldek continued its negative decline through the incredible misuse of power, control, and greed. Over time the remaining Maldekians became complacent and eventually surrendered their free will in exchange for food, work, shelter, entertainment, and infrequent rewards of self-creativity. Most willingly gave up and lost their individuality, allowing these governing forces to tell them what to do, and how to live as a collective people.

Subsequently, the Maldekian society grew even darker in its lovelessness and violence—and then finally used the science of cloning to create a perfected species without free will inclinations. These clones were not robots, yet they were created to obey and act on command as a species of workers, soldiers and protectors of the planet who maintained discipline within the citizenry. Their scientific experimentation with crystal chip devices capable of controlling and maintaining complacency among the citizenry was successfully implemented. Ultimately, the misuse of the powerful fire crystals set off a major component of the energy rod systems (similar to your nuclear missiles) and the Maldekians destroyed their own people and planet in a horrific explosion.

As mentioned, this explosion created your asteroid belt and also created a traumatic ripple effect throughout the galaxy and planetary systems. The Universal Overseers still did not want to interfere with the action of others, but they began monitoring the planetary systems closely to see if a collective species would again misuse and set off another nuclear holocaust. I want you to understand that many of your own people on Earth are in nearly the same consciousness vibration today as Maldek once was before its total destruction. Much of the Earth's population is becoming complacent, materialistic and loveless. Violence in thought and action is increasing daily. Misuse of power is so rampant in all walks of life that it is creating devastation on many levels throughout the planet.

In addition, your governments are creating horrific devices that can destroy the planet and civilization. High among the list of your worst dangers are atomic, nuclear, and biochemical warfare, as well as the psychotronic mind control devices using various frequencies which can cause mental, emotional and physical symptoms of chaotic behavior, even insanity.

Another potential disaster to your human lives and free will recently began with the increasing practice of unnatural cloning. Negative or unnatural cloning is a desecration of the natural law of creation. I recommend that this manipulative and non-spiritual process of cloning be abolished—and I will refer to cloning again in a later chapter. Always remember that implantation of chips or sophisticated devices, or the use of cloning procedures used to control innocent beings against their will, is a spiritually corrupt act, especially when a government enforces its will upon its citizens.

Humanity is fortunate today in that, regardless of any ignoble deeds, the higher celestials will not allow the Earth to be destroyed. There will, however, be a purification experience through nuclear activity, famine, and disease if humanity does not turn their hearts back to loving each other and their Creator.

Those peaceful Maldekians who left before the final explosion of their planet to reside on other spherical planetary systems were now under discussion in the greater councils of light. The council's decision was that these Maldekians and others who would follow, were permitted to colonize a new civilization upon planet Earth. Many from Maldek, Pleiades, Lyra, Andromeda, Venus and other systems left to start a new colonization of peace upon the planet Shawn now called Earth. This colonization began what you know as the Lemurian Epoch, which will be the subject of our next chapter.

But first, Virginia, do you have any questions?

* * *

VE: With gratitude I greet you once again, and thank you for this fascinating material. Could you please clarify more fully how the Venusian "integration chamber" works and tell us whether a building in southern California called the Integratron is either a forerunner or an example of it. Are similar ones on Earth now?

AM: What you call the Integratron was built according to scale by an Earth brother connected to the Venusian Council. This Integratron is one of the chambers that holds a life stream of energy connecting it to the Venusians. By utilizing the electro-magnetic fields in the dispersement and assimilation process, the energy can be used as a rejuvenation chamber. It is also a major vortex that connects to the Venusian thought banks for higher inter-dimensional knowledge, as well as to Earth's major sites and to various grid systems throughout your galaxy. This dome is on a time-released thought program, which means it is releasing information in specific time sequences to those within its walls who connect to its generated energy. It was designed to disperse and activate energy particularly for the healing and rejuvenation of the human form. This chamber was designed with energy rods placed in precise connection with the sphere interceptor chords of color, light and sound.

VE: Very interesting. Now in the chapter it wasn't explained whether the matriarchs of Clarion are exclusively androgynous or partnered with masculine beings. Also, have any great women in Earth's history been guided by these Clarion matriarchs?

AM: The matriarchs on the planet Clarion are androgynous, but hold the feminine nature of embodiment. They are also known as divine ministers who are working on higher mind techniques and the law of magnetic dynamics. They are bringing gifts of love through the vibration of telepathy to assist those women on Earth to stand strong and to use their gifts to balance the mental and emotional embodiments for wellness. The symbol that they hold and bring to Earth is the flowers of spring in order to nurture, comfort and bring the rebirthing of humanity into a glorious self-beautification. There have been many women on Earth who have had the gift of guidance from Clarion, bringing incredible gifts of insight and wisdom. Women were the first gifted shamans on your Earth and the Clarions assisted them in developing their wisdom, inner sight, and vision so that they could assist many other lives.

I will mention only a few of the millions of women influenced during your recorded history, such as Mother Mary, Mary Magdalene, Ruth, Joan of Arc, Mother Theresa, Grandma Moses, Amelia Earhart, Shirley Chisholm, Helen Keller, Eleanor Roosevelt, and so many others. Just look at the women who are strong in expressing their own area of expertise, in assisting other people and their country, and women who devote their lives to the betterment of their families and children. You will know them when you see them!

VE: Regarding your comments that there are pyramids on every planet, do we now have actual photographs of a pyramid on Mars? Are pyramids only needed in the physical dimensions or do they exist in the fifth dimension and above.

AM: The fifth dimension is a physical-etheric dimension, and pyramids do exist there as well as throughout other universes. However, outside of the boundaries of this Universe they will not appear in solid form as they do now on Earth and even upon Mars. On Mars, and all planetary systems, there are pyramids because these connectors of information, energy grids and landing stations hold sacred mathematical equations for the opening of the sacred portals using the chords of tone energy.

Pyramids in the higher celestial realms use incredible fire crystals that are formed with complex geometrical combinations. They hold intricate designs that are bejeweled with multiple precious fire gems, each holding a different mathematical language that is dispersed and interlaced with many pyramids throughout the worlds. They are far more wondrous than those of yours upon Earth and even those located within the fifth dimension.

VE: Since the Maldekians were allowed to blow up an entire planet and we humans seem capable of doing something similar—does that mean free will is an absolute privilege no matter how violently people behave?

AM: There are universal laws that must be kept, and we could not have interfered with the planet Maldek at that time. When Maldek destroyed itself, it caused a ripple effect that created a great devastation within the galaxy and affected many planetary systems. The Great Ones decided that in order to protect so many other dedicated beings, they would not allow another planet to destroy itself. Consequently, the Time Keepers have been told that they can maintain a balance in order to keep another planet from destruction. This is called a Divine Intervention, and allows many of our celestials to make themselves known to humanity. They appear as messengers, reminding humanity to awaken and to change its ways. Angels are coming to many people to help them reach higher states of being. I, Michael, am gathering the illuminators to wake up and become aware of their abilities in order to change the path of destruction. However, if humans continue on their destructive path, the Earth Mother herself will stop a total destruction by bringing humanity to its knees and back into humbleness. Earth is not going into a nuclear age; it is rising to a Solar Age. Humanity may have to go through a purification, but Earth will not be destroyed.

VE: With reference to our galaxy and Universe, can you explain what percentage of life exists in the third and fourth dimensions, compared to the fifth dimension and above?

AM: Can you count the multiple grains of sand upon your beaches? A calculated percentage would not be correct, because we do not separate. However, to give you an understanding, there are not as many Earths or physical planets as there are higher celestial worlds, so the higher worlds would far surpass the physical states of being. However, this does not make humans unimportant.

When we look upon humanity, we see it as a growing, blossoming flower. Even though some of the petals are dropping or the leaves are wilting, we know that it is about to be birthed again for another journey and another spring of growth and beauty.

> If you knew that wiser and loving civilizations had once colonized Earth and you felt a yearning for their wisdom and love, would you try to recover that inner knowing?

Chapter 7

Lemuria

Lest this technical information I'll be giving you about the Lemurian culture suggest that they led impersonal lives, I want to assure you that their lives were actually filled with harmonious love, extended family bonding, relationship with animals, extraordinary art and musical expression and entertainment. They lived for thousands of years without pain and suffering until some of them digressed into dense physical form. The Lemurians also experienced a joyful and creative life—a life which humans today would generally call heaven! It is this kind of existence that the awakening human species is now moving toward with soulful longing.

As previously mentioned, the Yananeenees and the Logos eras came and went long ago. Then there were physical-etheric beings who came from various celestial worlds such as Venus into the density of a beautiful physical-etheric planet called Shawn, which is now the denser physical planet called Earth. At that beginning colonization many of these higher beings came to reign on Earth and to establish a civilization that was eventually divided into many different provinces, such as Undul, Ur, and Poseidon. These provinces were part of a single Earth land mass with no major ocean separations. Each of these areas held unique levels of elevated thought in specific fields so that each being would perform specific duties and specialties at a high level of competency. Because these beings held physical-etheric bodies they communicated telepathically—not with voice as humanity does today. As you may know, telepathy is a language of thought frequencies that uses various components of color, light and sound, and is based on an energy we call the crystal fire language.

It's important to understand that not all beings were identical in their telepathic abilities because not all of them carried the same spiritual frequency or level of knowledge. Just as humans today have various levels of mind development—slow, methodical, alert, highly specialized or genius—so those beings were also unique. Each mind, wherever you exist, can learn and expand to an ever higher consciousness. So, at the time of Lemuria, even the higher beings still had many levels of continued growth and learning available, which is why they created specialized temples of intelligence to accommodate those differences.

By conversing mind to mind, the Lemurians had the power to design different mind frequency formulas that could instantaneously bring thoughts into physical form, thereby creating a spectacular crystal civilization. Amazing as it may seem today, by using the power of their minds in unison they created structures, schools, abodes and other places of wonder, yet each Lemurian held their own level of consciousness and expertise.

The more highly empowered Lemurians had the ability to think in unison and would gather in a circle envisioning the golden band of higher frequencies until their coded design came into form. By modulating and correlating their thoughts together to create a vibratory rate of frequency transcending the level where their physical-etheric bodies were situated, they would open the halls of sacred knowledge from their prior etheric worlds. When their thoughts connected together, that power created a circular or spherical band of electrical flow that would intra-penetrate through the universal magnetic fields and then assemble the knowledge. This data would then be transported back to them and their minds would solidify the thought frequencies into either one crystal, a cluster, or a composite of crystals. Once the information was placed within the facets of the crystal it remained there until the power was activated and the information released. Some of you are now remembering those times and long to regain these powers. (But power, without love, can be dangerous as you can see quite dramatically demonstrated on planet Earth today.)

RAINBOW TEMPLES OF HEALING

To maintain the necessary level of light frequency so they could remain embodied in a material, or physical, dimension, special apparatus had to be created for the Lemurians. These were called the Rainbow Temples of Healing and contained auric stabilizers that assisted them in staying etheric or helping them to keep their physical-etheric bodies stabilized. Unlike humans today, their bodies had to maintain a high level of light energy in order to keep balanced while on the lower plane of density. These Rainbow Temples were about 40 feet high with pyramid-shaped tops. Underneath these high tops was a circular foundation that had 15 foot crystals, with multiple facets, cut and inlaid into 12 major triangles, each triangle holding its own color vibration. Although separated into 12 sections, they all formed one concentric circle allowing alternating connections within the crystals. Each of the 12 triangle crystals could be broken down into 144,000 different healing formula combinations. So in essence, each of the original 12 large crystals held 144,000 different formulas to produce the light, color, and sound for healing.

The Rainbow Keepers or healers had to understand each of these 144,000 composites or variables of high energy patterns to do their work. When a Lemurian came to the rainbow healers for a healing session, the healers would use their telepathic ability to read the flow of energy from their client's auric light fields and also determine which levels of treatment would be necessary.

After reading the person's auric light fields, they would take the individual into the healing circle. In the middle of the healing room would be a solid alabaster cube on which the person would be placed. The healers would choose the correct combination of crystals to be activated telepathically and instantly a kaleidoscope of incredible colors would reflect beautiful melodious tones and a barrage of interlaced strobes of light currents. This array of musical tones created a symphony, which joined with the color currents to encircle the room. This interlacing combination of color and sound together created a vibrational frequency that would enhance the energy fields of the individual who was lying on the alabaster cube. The body would then receive the tone energy patterns and be re-energized into the higher frequencies of etheric light that would rejuvenate each low-vibrating organ back to a state of balance.

THE RAINBOW ARCHES

The Rainbow Keepers or healers were skilled in the ability to read the genetic coding of all Lemurians and could code either a triple or quadruple helix, or program whatever strands were required to establish the necessary changes. Inside of these domes were crystal cube-like cocoons or beds positioned next to each other on the inside wall. Over each of these cube stations or beds were energy rods shaped in an arch. These arched rods spread out over the beds approximately 1 to 2 feet apart, depending on the size of the beings—some of whom were 15-20 feet tall. These rods were set on floors that were inlaid with various configurations of crystals, which connected through a vibrational system to the arches of each of these beds. When a treatment was given the arched energy rods would lift up, the individual would step in and then lie down as the arches lowered to be locked into place.

In addition to genetic healing processes, these cocoons also had other uses. One use was to increase their telepathic capabilities by connecting them to appropriate grid stations in various planetary systems. The grid stations on Andromeda, Sirius, Arcturus, Saturn, Venus, Perseus, and Epsilon Böötes use a digital dot system to provide that mind frequency training.

THE ACCELERATION LEARNING CHAMBERS

Another higher level of Lemurian education took place in what was called the acceleration learning chambers. In somewhat the same way you on Earth have specialists, Lemuria had a broad range of citizens wise and loving enough to be the creators of civilizations. Other important and talented beings became the rulers, lawmakers, over-lords of provinces, scientists, mathematicians, astronauts, and technologists. Then there were the educators, specialized telepathic transmitters and receivers, crystalline orderlies, global communicators, mind group synchronizers, crystal creators/ keepers, and data organizers. In the field of healing in addition to the rainbow healers, there were also global physicians, auric stabilizers, group minds of the crystalline order (workers of radionics), telepathic musicians, sound and color healers, electro-magnetic guardians, and many others.

Because the Lemurians were at different levels of development, education was a major priority in the culture. Educators therefore played a crucial role in the Lemurian civilization, and they were in charge of the acceleration learning chambers. These acceleration chambers had circular and oval shapes, depending on the dynamics of teachings tools used, and there were different chambers used for a variety of subjects. Since Lemurians had different levels of telepathic abilities there were beings who were empowered as overseers because they held incredible mind power dynamics.

The acceleration chambers were used by many educators who had the ability to read the mind-set of those who would come to them. They could then measure the functioning capabilities of the student's telepathic brilliance to see if the student was ready to be programmed into the next step of advanced study or learning. The students would be taken to an acceleration room that had multiple chairs lined up, similar to your schoolrooms, but these chairs were made out of a precious metal called tolitium. Tolitium is not a metal that you on Earth are aware of at this time, but it was used during Lemuria and Atlantis as one of their primary metals. Connected onto the back of each chair was a large helmet that was used as a conductor of energy and that stabilized the vibrational ranges of frequencies to be activated. The helmet had geometrical indentations placed on the front and back, and since the educators already knew the next level the student could attain, they would collect the necessary geometrically designed fire crystals and place them into the indentations upon the helmet.

As the learner sat under the helmet he/she would stimulate the crystals by mind power, activating them into a wonderful kaleidoscope of sound and color. The mind would then telepathically absorb the energy patterns and assimilate the information into the brain, gaining a greater range of memory and workable mind abilities in its particular field of interest. This was just one of the many ways in which a Lemurian was schooled into higher levels of intelligence—just as humans today go from elementary school, possibly college, or specialized schools.

The children of Lemuria were schooled in a more elementary level, of course. The master educators would ask them to sit in a circle and tell them to concentrate on a geometrical circle. As they did this, it was essential to keep their minds absolutely focused in a one-mind frequency. If any one of them became distracted it would break the harmony pattern of concentration required for what the whole group was attempting to accomplish. Then they would have to keep trying until they could hold the unified thought of a geometrical circle and keep the rhythm of that frequency until the geometrical circle actually solidified into the form of a physical ball. When their minds accomplished this feat they would learn to throw the ball back and forth, still holding the energy pattern of thought. This helped them to develop their power of kinetic energy.

The children were exhilarated by this playful but serious accomplishment, knowing that they were beginning to develop their cosmic mind techniques of communication. As these children grew, each would become specialized in the particular field in which their talents began to manifest. Some would work primarily on their own as individuals, some paired with partners, while others would have the capability to work together with a cosmic mind group. As an active unit within a group mind, they eventually would travel, work, and even live together.

The artists of Lemuria could instantly crystallize thought into clusters of crystals that would be placed into a geometrical configuration of absolute precision. As it was inlaid into a piece of metal it would then become a piece of art. Just as many of your artists today see a vision of abstract colors within their minds, the Lemurians compiled their pieces of artwork to keep the harmonics of their homes and tabernacles balanced. They were deeply aesthetic and truly enjoyed creating these extraordinary images.

In the same way, the musicians and other creative beings also made great contributions to society's aesthetic and cultural needs.

PROCREATION IN LEMURIA

Because family was a truly meaningful experience in the Lemurian culture, children were genuinely loved and treasured. Their method of conceiving a child was very different from how humans create offspring. Lemurian children were birthed when the masculine and feminine energies of a group would join together and embrace each other through their mind energies. As they came together they held a pattern of thought that would elevate them in a complete union with each other. As this union took place they would reach an ecstasy of togetherness within their harmonic activity which produced a genetic replication—the seeding of an energy composite of themselves. This energy composite was instantly birthed as a seed of light that was placed into incubation for a time.

While in the crystal incubator the child-to-be would be monitored by its cosmic family who would overview it and make sure it was receiving the correct energy patterns until it was fully developed. When the time came for the birthing of the child, they all gathered together in mind unison and when they opened the crystal container the child would amazingly already be matured to the level of a 12-year-old Earth child. The child would then be taken to the head council where instructions were given as to where it would begin life. A plan would be made for its telepathic development and growth. Depending on the purpose for the child's creation, this birthing could be done in groups, or even by sets of two. There were also specialized nursing caretakers who assisted in caring for these wondrous offspring.

Later on, when the Lemurian civilization divided into two groups, those who retained the purity of oneness continued this pattern of procreation. However, the group that separated and became Atlantis eventually intermingled with the physical beings already on Earth which began their descent into the density of matter.

HALLS OF THE CRYSTALLINE ORDER

Like your present day libraries, the crystals that held solidified thought on many cosmic subjects were kept in the Halls of the Crystalline Order. They had information on intergalactic and celestial systems, mapping systems, travel data, science, mathematics, technology, philosophy, literature, telepathy and mind development, language, aeronautics and light ships. These individual specialties were housed in different crystal halls scattered throughout Lemuria's many provinces.

The Lemurian buildings were created by higher technologists and architects in group mind unison. They used their telepathic abilities to envision a geometrical configuration or design of the various buildings that they chose to create. Some buildings were circular or oval, while others were shaped as a pyramid. Each geometrical design was meticulously placed together in order for the power of the solar rays and the lunar rays to energize the angles of the building for the storing and usage of the fire crystals.

Because some of the Lemurians had the telepathic ability to open the higher records held in the celestial dimensions from which they had come, they could still bring knowledge to Lemuria and manifest it into a solid crystal configuration. Those beings who were the transmitters and receivers of information from the sacred vaults stored in the galactic systems belonged to the Amethystine Order. Members of this order were the mathematicians, architects, builders, priests, and engineers who would sit in a circle and in unison think of a geometrical picture. They had the ability to instantly create what they held together in their minds and were able to manifest the blueprint into matter. All of Lemuria and the provinces were created by the higher technologists who used the power of their minds to tap into the electro-magnetic fields, through the windows of infrared and gamma rays, to solidify their thought patterns. Many of the pyramids, megalithic and monolithic structures that exist even today were built by the Amethystine Order.

Other Lemurians were trained in specific fields so that someone who was highly gifted with the grids, or could utilize the galactic mapping systems, would be able to telepathically open his/her mind to the information that had been accumulated. He/she would then project the mind's knowledge into a solidified piece of crystal, a cluster of crystals, or a particular configuration of crystals. These crystals would then be placed into the Crystalline Halls of Order to be kept until needed. The subject variations of these crystals were immense, similar to the knowledge contained in your own libraries and computers.

THE CRYSTALLINE KEEPERS

There were certain Lemurians who had the ability to keep the crystals in their appropriate order, similar to your librarians today, but these keepers also had to have the ability to read the auric pattern of those who came and wanted to check the crystals out for purposes of learning. Since the learner had to have the correct mind power to activate the crystals, if their mind wasn't ready, the crystal would not be of any use to them. It was these Crystalline Keepers who had to read the auric vibration of the person's mind to determine if the material was appropriate. If it was, the learner was taken to a special room which had been created to sustain the vibration of the knowledge that was contained in that particular crystal. These learners would hold the crystal in their hands and activate the crystal with their mind. The crystal would then resonate an incredible kaleidoscope of color and sound throughout the room and the information was then absorbed through the learner's memory cells for immediate use. If the keepers saw that the learner was not ready, they would advise what other crystal unit could be used, or suggest some training in a particular educational dome to better prepare the learner to assimilate the information being sought.

Many of the crystals were given to the educators to be used in the acceleration helmets. As mentioned, these helmets were used for higher education, especially for the beings who had been schooled in using the crystals individually, and could now withstand the frequency impact of the combinations of energy received by their mind.

WHEELS OF MECHANIZATION

In any great technical civilization interplanetary travel is a major activity. In Lemuria they had built special crafts called Vimana ships that were used for traveling throughout space-time to other planetary systems. Some of the ships were silent while others held melodious sound. The astronauts who were trained to utilize navigational fire crystals for flight would place various programmed fire crystals into the portholes inside their circular ships. In unison, the flight technicians would telepathically activate the fire crystals to create a propulsion effect, which through the high-powered resonating vibrations, would tap into an energy called *ether*—an ethereal substance. This would cause a gravitational force or hydrostatic pressure that fueled the ships and allowed them to maneuver through grid formations of space. The fire crystals that were used for fuel gave an incredible radiant energy from the Sun that was utilized for traveling throughout the interstellar constellations.

The interstellar mapping systems were also contained within the various configurations of crystals and each ship was given both a directory of crystal formations, according to their destination, and galactic mapping data to interface with the commanders of each dimensional station. Even today your airplanes and airports have computerized monitoring and radar equipment for commercial flights, not to mention the military technical equipment— some of which has expanded into your early space travel. It is likely that those of you reading this material may have used some of these specialties in prior times. These Vimana ships were extraordinary vehicles for space travel because they were built to use the geometrical law of motion dynamics, which permitted oblong, triangular and circular shapes to move in very precise flight maneuvers. These geometrical designs had angles holding a hidden power that would enmesh with the fire crystals and assist with the latent mercury fueling agent.

THE ANIMAL WORLD OF LEMURIA

During the Lemurian era there were many animal beings that roamed the Earth, but two quite unique animal forms who were closely united with the Lemurians were the lions and the group called whales and dolphins. Other animals were created during Earth's natural evolutionary cycles, but the lions, whales and dolphins came to Earth from the celestial realms. Of the many beings in feline form at that time the lions were truly spectacular for they had telepathic abilities that connected to the souls and minds of their families through an incredible bond of love. In fact, many of these unique felines came with the physical-etheric beings who entered Earth's vibration from the higher planetary systems.

The lions migrated around Earth with their families through various stages of life in Lemuria, Atlantis, and even early Egypt. In fact, the Sphinx is a symbol of these divine beings. Unbelievable as it may seem, these lion entities were actually from future worlds. Imagine if you can a handsome lion body standing upright, tall and majestic in appearance. The face had an elongated nose, firmly set jaw, pointed ears and wide crystal blue eyes that could scan through the veils of both past and future times. This particular lion-like species was very wise and utilized the tablets of the light crystal worlds and passages. Later, some of these beings who chose to come to Lemuria, discovered they had to rearrange their higher light bodies into a lion-like form that was no longer capable of standing in an upright position. So they eventually appeared as four-legged animal beings even though they were not.

Even in this form they were very telepathic and remembered their former planetary knowledge. They united strongly with the various cosmic families and assisted in creating the ley lines, or routes, that would connect to the light crystal worlds from which they came. This allowed them to enter and exit different dimensions as needed. These lion-like beings stayed with the celestials of Lemuria and migrated with them through Atlantis and into early Egypt.

When the celestials began to digress and had to go through the incarnational pattern of the Earth plane, their lion companions chose to stay connected and agreed that they, too, would come back and join them during the various life experiences of their Earth journey. Thus it was that the Lemurians and Atlanteans, when building the pyramids of Egypt, also erected the Sphinx in honor of these beings from the crystal light worlds of the future. When you see a picture of a sphinx, look upon it as a memorial symbol honoring higher beings who are your future worlds.

In later Egypt, during the dynasties, felines were held in high esteem. In fact, many of the panthers, leopards, and lions were trained for the protection of personal homes and lives. Because of the majestic strength and courage that these animals held, they were also known as temple cats and were greatly admired. Some of these big cats agreed to come back later in a smaller cat form just to be companions with those from previous life times. So if you have a cat that has found its way to you it could be one of your companions who had been with you in the early times of Lemuria, Atlantis, Egypt, or another celestial system.

These modern cats help neutralize emotional upsets or physical discomforts. That is why some of your cats will position themselves on your chest, or sleep close to you. Also, some can send telepathic messages to those who are sufficiently conscious to recognize that they have come back.

Lemurians were involved with another highly developed species, those mammals you call cetaceans—the whales and dolphins. These highly-developed spiritual beings did not evolve from Earth's natural evolutionary process, but were sent from the higher councils with the Lemurians, and with later human generations, also. I know that this may seem difficult for some people to believe, but these are highly developed beings that come from another world in time.

Although they have very different bodies than yours, whales and dolphins are connected directly to the higher systems throughout your Universe by their sonar language. They create amazing melodious tones for healing, and they maintain a vibratory rate that has a positive effect on many of the portals and entrances that connect Earth's Inner Worlds and your celestial heavens. They also relay information to the celestial systems regarding the progress of your Earth, the shifting of your ocean floors, the movement of Earth's tectonic plates and her subterranean cities. The special vibrations of the dolphins emit healing properties for humans but most particularly during a human infant's birth process. Dolphins especially love the vibration of children and have been known to save humans beings when they have experienced a dangerous event in the ocean.

The whales and dolphins are connected together cosmically and are cooperating during the changes on Earth. Long ago, some dolphins and whales agreed in their collective spirit to stay on Earth and become transmitters and receivers of information about the consciousness of humanity. As the human consciousness is beginning to shift to a more negative vibration, the cetaceans are choosing to leave the Earth plane.

This is happening right now because of humanity's incredible abuse and slaughter of these divine creations. Some whales are beaching themselves in order to leave their earthly bodies because they are being harmed by underwater military experiments that negatively affect their vibrational fields. Please do not harm these magnificent beings because they are one of God's helpers and are supporting your planet's welfare at this ascension time. Love them, for they have all been created within the divine plan, and they also hold the eternal life force pulsation called breath just as you do.

It is a daunting task to try to explain the entire Lemurian culture with its many exciting and unusual components, but perhaps this brief introduction will be helpful as humanity moves into higher consciousness and more open perceptions. I hope these descriptions of an influential and positive civilization will release inspiration and joy in your hearts because some of you reading these words still carry the influences and attributes of that former time and place.

Now, Virginia, have you some questions you would like to ask at his time?

* * *

VE: Greetings once again and please accept our gratitude for this informative material on Lemuria. The description you have given about the Lemurian's Vimana ships raises the issue of aliens and UFO's—something you haven't discussed thus far in the book. Can you give us your perspective on the Lemurians who traveled in spacecraft and who must have been "alien"— as compared to the aliens and the UFO spacecraft we see today? What is humanity's role in all this and what should our response be to their presence? How can we evaluate who is ethical and who is not?

AM: There are over 650 million planets that have life on them within your galaxy alone. The higher beings who came and created civilizations long ago on Earth had come from the higher worlds of the celestial dimensions, and they are the beings that you refer to as aliens today. Many of these celestials have various assignments as the angelic messengers who have appeared and delivered messages to mankind throughout the eras of time. The Bible and other beautiful inspired writings have spoken about the higher celestials, the celestial planes of existence, wheels within wheels and their mode of travel. The celestials who have appeared to many humans illumine an incredible light force, which led humans to think that they had wings, but this is not so. It is a stream of light, a propulsion system, allowing them to transport from one realm of existence to another.

When you meet an angel/celestial of light you are enfolded with its beauty and divine essence of love. Light does not manipulate, enforce or compel people against their will. There are many different levels of aliens, just as there are many different levels of humans. If you are encountering these beings, then you may have had an agreement long ago to come back at this time to assist them in their development. Some physical aliens are now on Earth to cause an intrusion by interfering with humanity, and are scientifically experimenting not only with humans and your animals, but are also involved with your affairs of state. These beings are concerned primarily for the advancement of their own species by connecting genetically with the human race.

Aliens who hold the lower nature patterns do cause unrest, wars, intrusion, and discomfort. These aliens want to manipulate humans and confine them into imprisonment through the use of sophisticated devices of control. Remember you are working out of the current physical illusion into the worlds of the living light, and you will knowingly be able to discern the negative forces from those who come to assist in the uplifting of humanity and its consciousness.

VE: How close are we to having some of the Lemurian healing equipment you mentioned?

AM: Many are now coming into the greater capacity of utilizing higher technologies for healing. But until Earth and her population uplift into a higher vibratory rate, you will not be able to use the fire crystals as they did in Lemuria. However, there are those who are using miniscule replicas based on their memory of these great chambers of healing. Some healers are using crystals again for multiple purposes, because crystals still hold some vibrancy of the knowledge that was used long ago and will be used again. Crystals have become very predominate in the past 25 years because many people are awakening to those memories of old.

Another way of utilizing Lemurian healing techniques is by using color therapy. Some of you are creating domes, using the spectrum of the color rays placed around a circular room. These colors of red, orange, yellow, green, blue, indigo blue, and violet connect to the chakras, and therefore connect to each of the governing districts of your body's organs. Sitting under each of these seven lights for an interval of five minutes while meditating brings healing and relaxation to the physical, mental, and emotional bodies. The one very powerful healing process you all can use today is focusing the mind to create healing imagery.

There are many technical devices such as the Rife machine, and other healing instruments, that utilize both the electromagnetic fields and magnetic energy as a source of healing. Many tools and techniques of utilizing the mastery of sound energy are also being revived. These tools and techniques include vocal expressions such as toning and chanting as well as playing instruments that emanate healing musical chords. Sound heals by lifting the vibratory rate of the body organ into a higher energy of balance.

This is a brief answer, but it would not be possible to mention all the sophisticated ways in which many humans on Earth are being awakened for the purposes of healing. More and more are continuing to open their minds and create more inventive instrumentation to assist humanity. *Remember, the greatest healer is the power of your own mind in overcoming the obstacles of self by connecting to the Source within, which is the ultimate source for healing.*

VE: Do you see humanity creating any of the educational technical devices the Lemurians had?

AM: Humans cannot create the same educational chambers as were used in Lemuria, because, as mentioned, you do not have the capacity to utilize the fire crystal methods. The Lemurians were highly telepathic beings who knew how to utilize the particles of the Sun, such as infrared rays, gamma rays and others in order to instantly manifest their desires by using their minds.

You star beings are now beginning to awaken and develop the mind-to-mind abilities, but your use is still very limited compared to what was used in Lemuria. However, there are ways in which you are developing higher mind techniques and telepathically connecting with your teachers, angels, and aliens, who will be giving more knowledge of greater techniques. Also, you are learning how to connect with your own power of mind and are using this power to bring forward your own levels of development and answers.

Your schools of learning are utilizing computers, which is one of the advanced ways in which children of Earth are being taught. However, the educators are forgetting that the computer cannot take the place of a human because the emotional element of the body requires personal energy exchange and contact. Human contact is a very important ingredient in nurturing, comforting, praising, and assuring the child's needs are met.

Many children are star children, and they are connecting during this time to the sophisticated computer processes and computer language with ease. However, the greatest tool is mind, and this needs to be developed by being exposed to educational practices using color, sound, group mind togetherness, and imagery. Education should allow students to discover what gives them joy in learning, and to assist in the development of their particular abilities. Your educational facilities and teaching methods do not generally allow the freedom of expression, but maintain a level of structured conformity that dulls the imagination and the ability to develop latent skills. Regrettably, many courses using the imagination in the arts, theatre, and music are being reduced to a minuscule experience. Consequently, many star children will be seeking the teachers who will be using techniques in mind development, creative exploration and self-expression.

VE: What percentage of humanity is using some form of telepathy or the pictography language?

AM: There are many different degrees of telepathy, and you on Earth are in the beginning stages of this development. Multiple levels of telepathic thought are used through the windows of imagery, vision, and inspiration. Your artists see pictures, perhaps futuristic scenes that are not from this world, that create a stir within them to be painted. Musicians can hear symphonic chords that must be creatively transformed to a composition to be played and appreciated. Lyricists hear words that must be sung. Inventors see new inventions that can assist humanity and writers and philosophers are bringinga new way of thinking to advance the consciousness of humanity. Creativity is greatly expanding everywhere.

The pictography language cannot be used by many at this time. As an example of what pictography is, I can use my thought ability to observe and extract instantly all thought equations of beings throughout many systems of light simultaneously. You on Earth will be capable of developing a telepathic language that will escalate the advanced degrees of mind-to-mind abilities as you grow and mature in your spiritual endeavors.

VE: Please give us your perspective on humanity's entrance into space travel. Are we ethical enough to be trusted out there?

AM: Humankind has the ability to travel through space to a certain degree, but you are still very limited in the technology necessary to traverse into higher dimensions. The celestials are monitoring Earth and will allow many humans to have interval sightings. Humankind will awaken and know that they are not alone. Many celestials have already made contact with you, and many more will be seen to erase any doubt that humanity may have so they can assist when the time is correct. However, for now, humanity has not spiritually evolved enough in order to safely use the higher technology.

As to whether you are ethical enough to be trusted to travel through space, one must simply observe humanity as we do. Already humans have demonstrated their destructive ways of using higher technologies on Earth by controlling, manipulating and destroying their own humankind. Therein lies the answer to your question.

Chapter 8
Migration to Atlantis and Egypt

Life is ever changing, and so it was that over a period of time the different groups who colonized Lemuria began to have disputes because some wanted to misuse the fire crystal energy. Eventually the Lemurians' energy of a stable collective consciousness began to separate, dividing Lemuria into two units of conscious beings. Since there was only one continuous land surface or continent, the migration was easy to do.

One group we shall call the Lemurians used the higher technologies in a balanced way and kept themselves in harmony with their spirituality of Oneness. This society maintained peace and worked together in great unity, using their crystal knowledge for the betterment of their civilization as they related with the higher worlds.

The second group, which chose the way of compelling, enforcing and misusing the knowledge of the fire crystals, became those you call the Atlanteans. Just as the Maldekians had previously done, some of the higher technologists and scientists began creating life by negative cloning. They sought to perfect a genetic race of beings lacking God consciousness, who would assist in menial tasks.

The Atlantean overseers of these clones controlled the clones by the implantation of crystal chips placed in back of their skulls, necks, noses and ears. If a clone wasn't orderly and went against the rules, it would be incarcerated. Once the clones had these chips or rods implanted, of course, they had no more freedom because any thought that registered a vibration against the governing system would trigger the chip or rod to render mental confusion or even cause a temporary stupor. The mind control device worked by reorganizing the frequency patterns of their thinking capabilities. If there was an action being manifested by a group or an individual that was against the frequency maintained within the implanted chip, it would pierce the brain with accelerated activity and create immobility. In this way, the chips or needle-like rods were used to control civil disobedience among their own citizenry.

Later on, the scientists of Atlantis warred against all opposition and began experimenting with clusters of crystals, rearranging and redistributing them throughout the land, which caused a disruption in the planet's stability. The original crystals that had been installed in the Earth by the Lemurians had stabilized vortices of energy, helping them hold their own physical-etheric vibration, and also maintaining a necessary communication with higher dimensions. Because of the Atlantean's immoral disregard for life, when they foolishly experimented with the fire energy crystals, they caused an upset in both the electro-magnetic and the bio-gravitational fields of Earth. This distorted energy caused the planet to disembowel with tremendous earthquakes causing the Earth's convulsion into separate continents and the two great bodies of water now called the Pacific and the Atlantic oceans.

Before this total destruction of Atlantis, many of the Lemurians, who were not in agreement with the Atlantean's misconduct and improper usage of the great crystals, began to migrate. These Lemurians were also joined by some of their Atlantean brothers who did not agree with what was happening. This combined group was asked by the higher beings to migrate across the entire planet's surface and create schools and storehouses of knowledge, landing stations, and grid vortices. Today you know these worldwide powerful temples as pyramids.

Although many humans don't realize it, there have always been pyramids elsewhere in your galaxy and beyond. So it is not surprising that some of you are fascinated by these pyramids and seek to understand their meaning and use. You see, for thousands of years the physical-etheric beings reigned upon Earth and built their civilizations throughout your planet, which is why you have found many pyramids throughout all land masses still above water—and why many are underneath the great oceans and seas. Each of these great pyramids was connected to the others through a very sophisticated grid system, called the spider web ley lines about which I have already spoken.

These pyramids were built not only to hold energy vortices throughout the Earth, but also the invisible inter-galactic mapping systems of energy lines connecting to many of the inter-galactic worlds. You may already know such worlds as Epsilon Böötes, Pleiades, Saturn, Venus, Sirius, the Inter-Galactic Headquarters of Arcturus and many others. Each of these locations or planetary systems holds a particular vibration, and they all dynamically interlace with each other and with the other pyramids that exist throughout all systems of the Universe. The pyramids contain symmetrical/geometric mathematics that are calculated to create barriers when necessary, or to allow the flow of thought to be transmitted from one station to another.

The physical pyramids are simply an exterior shell, but the interior vibration of what the pyramids truly hold is remarkable. Why? Because they are the megalithic structures that were designated and placed in the beginning of Lemuria as marked landing and communication stations. The higher beings knew of the energy contained within these invisible vortices and they used them when entering and exiting your Earth.

Once inside the inner worlds, accessed through the pyramids, there was a mechanism for teleportation within the Earth by travelling through tubes of light from one pyramid to another. Because the tubes of light did not work on the linear time frame, but in space-time of induced energy, it was easy for the Lemurians to communicate and travel within the Earth to any of the space landing stations (pyramids). In addition, there was space travel from the Earth to the outer worlds of existence through use of the previously mentioned Vimana ships. There was also an orbital evaluator, which was a hand-held device that telepathically re-arranged the molecular vibration of the body allowing instant teleportation beyond Earth into inter-dimensional realms.

In your movies and television programs you have your Star Trek kinds of adventures. However, as yet their producers have not said that we higher beings are very busy creating magnificent worlds for those of you on Earth who are spiritually able to lift up your cellular vibration to a molecular frequency. One day many of you will be able to open and walk through some of these entrances yourself, for there are many such portals throughout the Earth now and more are being activated. This is the genuine space adventure for which you yearn, beloved ones—the one you will achieve through wisdom and love!

As you gaze upon Earth's visible pyramids today, please realize there is an inverted etheric form of the pyramids beneath the soil that can take you into another vibration or plane of experience that I have already mentioned as the Holographic Computer and Inner World cities.

One of the greater entrances is at Giza, at the feet of the Sphinx, where the higher beings had the telepathic ability to raise their vibrational pattern and see the doorways to the other worlds. This technique is called Lute-sesame, melodious flute-like tones that create various patterns of sound in different octaves that would open the entrance. Wherever such a doorway opened it revealed a pyramidal solar light energy illuminating the corridor to the center beneath the pyramid, and to an entrance to another world vibration.

Those beings who could open the pyramids would meet with the elders at the center of the Earth in appropriate areas to help maintain the fire energy for building future temples, schools of learning, and also to receive initiations of higher development. These elders or golden ones are the wise executives chosen to maintain and utilize the Holographic Computer placed within the Earth's inner dimensional world at the time of Earth's creation. And they are still helping humanity today.

As time passed in the Lemurian-Atlantean saga, many of the Lemurians and even some Atlanteans who didn't agree with continuing misuse of the fire crystal power began migrating to a region known to humanity as Egypt. Here they began to create additional pyramids and temples while still retaining their ability to travel through space-time. The pharaohs, winged matriarchal pharaohs, priests and priestesses, and priest-craft (sacred mathematicians) were physical-etheric beings sometimes referred to as "the sons and daughters of God" who reigned during the early epochs of this civilization.

One of the most illustrious beings of this era was Thoth, who was an extraordinary scientist, philosopher, and bringer of the Emerald Tablet teachings. He was also the architect of major pyramids such as Giza and Cheops in cooperation with the pyramidologists from Epsilon Böötes. Because he met with the elders for various initiations they granted him immortality—a gift which he used to influence Egypt for thousands of years prior to the dynasties.

I am going to share with you something about two of these major pyramidal rooms in which many of the high beings, such as Thoth, used in their work. One of these rooms was circular in nature and was bathed in a beautiful glowing light far beyond the light that you have on the Earth at this time. In this light there is never any dimness of the divine light that continues to expand as conscious beings graduate to higher frequencies. The floor was crystal fire lighting and the ceiling was a canopy of active transparent grids and ley lines connecting to outer space, inner space and to the connecting vortices upon the surface of Earth. This particular room was a meeting place for various councils and also where the sons and daughters of God gathered together in communion. Here they were able to work the inter-stellar mapping system so essential to space travel.

The second room was used for storing star crafts of circular, triangular, and oblong design—and many other ships that were used to travel through space. As mentioned, some ships used hydrostatic pressure, or the universal substance called ether. There was also the Atlantean air power that utilized fire crystals to create a whirlwind vortex of generated power through the vibration of sound and color. Contrary to your movie versions of life in Egypt, there were highly advanced beings that reigned there during the pre-dynasty period.

These Lemurians and Atlanteans were the red-skinned giants who came from the worlds beyond the Earth plane. These beings, who are now designated as Egyptians, also began erecting mystery schools. They chose to intermingle with the sons and daughters of man—the physical species that had developed by natural evolutionary processes. They taught them how to use the language of mathematics, so they could learn to build physical structures. Eventually, some were taken into the sacred teaching of the pyramids, but only the pyramids above the surface of Earth. Humans were not able to raise their vibration to go into the invisible sacred halls beneath the pyramids.

As time went by many of the physical-etheric beings (the sons and daughters of God) were falling in love (desire) with the beautiful earthly creations (the sons and daughters of man) and wanted to encounter the physical realm of feeling and emotion. Therefore, many of the sons and daughters of God met with the elders beneath the great pyramids and told them that they wanted to stay and mate with the sons and daughters of man. However, there were a number of the sons and daughters of God who left Earth and chose to remove the fire crystals that maintained the etheric balance because they realized that the Lucifer vibration of duality would now be causing separation of life on Earth. It wasn't just the physical-etheric beings of Egypt choosing to leave, however, but all physical-etheric beings located everywhere on the planet.

As they departed with the fire crystals, they decided to activate an invisible rope-like band of light or force field that would encircle the outer perimeter of the planet. This meant that Earth's inhabitants would have to enter the karmic wheel of incarnation until they could raise their vibration to match the energy of the crystal band of light and graduate.

For those who chose to stay, the wise elders reminded them that if they chose this path they would genetically digress and become engulfed in the vibration of density. The elders further advised that they would acquire a new identity called the "star seeds" of Earth that would continue until humanity's ascension to the next higher world. If they stayed now they would be trapped on Earth, unable to leave the third dimension until ascension occurred. Nonetheless, knowing that they would have to experience death and stay only upon the Earth experiencing emotion and feeling, they chose density—with one safeguard.

They went before the council of light and agreed to put everything they knew of higher dimensional existence into a "fail-safe" system—a sophisticated crystal orb. They coded the fail-safe orb to be decoded at appropriate intervals as they went through the physical experiences of a denser vibration. This coded orb would later awaken them so they could use a particular gift to help the earthlings grow into a higher consciousness. Of course, in that particular life experience they would not recall that they were from the stars, but they would remember the gift of spirit so powerfully that they could not forget that divine part of themselves.

Thus it was that those who chose to begin the reincarnation process on Earth collectively vowed that they would come back to a total remembrance of their true identity during the end times. They would begin to use the available gifts of spirit to rebuild a new and better world. At the beginning they knew that they wouldn't remember each other for a long while, but eventually they would meet again by using their inner feeling to identify each other. Indeed, you have already had a deep feeling of knowing someone before, have you not?

Some of the beings chose to give one of their loved ones a key, or a part of their gift, to hold until a future time when they would meet to create and manifest their ideas. This was done so that the power could not be misused. No one would be allowed to remember the fail-safe plan or find all the keys for putting their knowing into action until they crossed each other's paths in a time frame called the latter days. Remember that when they made this fail-safe decision they were actually seeing every life incarnation and experience they would have until their later re-awakening. When the latter days came they would join together again with each other and with the higher councils of light. In the awakening moment of reconnection they would create another kind of a world—one of peace, love and joy.

As the latter days are now beginning, the present opportunity of the upcoming group ascension offers a collective gift of grace for humans and Earth. When planet Earth's own vibrational frequency increases to match the crystal band's force field, she too will pass into the fifth world. The great excitement in the heavens and on Earth is because a simultaneous expansion of many worlds will occur, allowing a long-awaited cosmic evolution to come closer to divine realization.

You have already read about many of these beings called star seeds who awakened to their previously encoded gifts in different time periods of history. Some beings would see incredible symbols of light and various color rays of beauty to be expressed even when the religious authorities would not allow them to be painted or when they would be destroyed because the art was supposedly heretical. Of course, at that time the collective consciousness of humanity was incredibly primitive and was caught up in the limitation of religious dogma. Nevertheless the artist's soul knew that, in time, humankind would see these paintings and the images would open their minds and hearts to a higher thought or concept through its visual power.

There were also great musicians who would hear incredible melodious tones in their minds and feverishly work to get the music into a composition to be played or sung. Sometimes the music was appreciated, other times not. However, the musicians couldn't deny the cosmic impulses to keep creating music. In the same way, other specialized gifts to be awakened or decoded within a special time frame brought forth scientists, philosophers, saints and spiritual leaders, writers, educators, and healers.

Eventually the seeds that were planted created a great stir in the hearts of many people, through many centuries of time. Few star seeds received the recognition for their work and gifts at the time of their endeavor, but it was meant to be that way. They were simply being the divine instruments in bringing higher thought, peace and understanding to raise the consciousness of humanity. In each case the soul knew why it had come and why it chose to undergo the limitations placed upon it by the existing nature of the various social environments. During these times, most people were ruled by the hands of fear, war and violence, and were controlled by religious organizations professing to be an acting authority of God. However, let me remind you that fear is not the nature of God, though it is the tool of Lucifer.

For those of you reading these words please honor who you are and why you have come to the planet because you are very likely these same physical-etheric beings who encoded your memories during the pre-dynasty Egyptian era.

And now let us pause for some of your questions, Virginia.

* * *

VE: Greetings to you once more as we gratefully continue to absorb your celestial information. Your description about the crystal chips implanted by the Atlanteans and Maldekians made me shudder because such things are starting here on Earth. What is our wisest response to this use of implants?

AM: *Do not take these implants into your physical embodiments.* Remember, there are those on Earth at this time who again desire to control the people as they did long ago. They want to take away the freedom people have to be the governing source of their own decisions and their own wisdom. Light does not compel. Light wants to empower you to come back into your own self-mastery, self-attainment and self-sovereignty—not for you to be ruled by implants. Of course, whatever choice you make, you must be responsible for your own actions.

VE: Along that same line, is cloning by our scientists and technologists advisable for humans or animals? Is it ever appropriate between species? And if a human is cloned, will it be left soul-less?

AM: This is a vast inquiry with many parts so let me begin by clarifying some basic definitions regarding humanity's God-given reproductive process.

As I mentioned in chapter 5, your human DNA/RNA double helix signature is God-given and holds a remarkable spiritual code. This code or unique genetic program has physical and non-physical data and requires the combined genetic information of the male sperm and the female ovum to spark the beginning of human life. This is natural reproduction. Obviously, a female could use the sperm of an unknown male donor and still meet those criteria.

Let me now list what is *not* appropriate for any genetic experiments so there can be no confusion among your scientists.

1. No single gene/cell exchange!
2. No combination of male to male or female to female codes!
3. No mixing different species such as humans and animals, animals with different animals, animals with vegetables, and so on.

Any of these genetic combinations produce harmful and unhealthy results.

There is another side of cloning which involves creating an identical replication by using the exact DNA sequence through genetic engineering. There are several reasons for these replication experiments that were done in Maldek and Atlantis. Scientists were primarily misusing their power by attempting to create the perfect superior race. They also wanted to have clones, such as servomechanisms and humanoids, merely to serve themselves. Although this was considered an erroneous act by the Universal Agents many such clones were created for those selfish desires. Later on, by God's mercy these cloned beings were later granted soul energy and allowed to join the human species.

We hear your bio-technologists and scientists saying that nature is always experimenting and creating new life forms so we can do the same. While this argument has some truth, remember that nature causes no accidental or deliberate harm and suffering in her evolving genetic intervention! Until humanity can say the same about its motives it is best to leave creation to God and the cosmic helpmates who are responsible for such things.

Please understand that there are many different ways in which the Source utilizes its breath process for birthing life forms throughout its many universes. *Although every life is created genetically through a unique coding system, the life of the entire species must hold the cells/genes of its planet's vibratory code and be birthed by the God breath intact.* Know that you tamper with this genetic design at the cost of your own spiritual consciousness!

VE: Thanks so much. What is the approximate number or percentage of star seeds, star lights and star children on Earth today? How many are awakened?

AM: Many of the star seeds, star lights and star children are awakening, even more so now that the tides of change become more apparent. The unveiling of memory is being activated, so that there will be more awareness of the higher heavens, the celestials and their part in the changing times. As a rough estimation, using the current world population, approximately one quarter of the souls are awakening at this time.

VE: Please explain how we could see every incarnation and experience on Earth when we sealed information in our "fail-safe" system's crystal orb. This suggests that everything is preplanned, just fated without possible change or creative adjustment. What about free will?

AM: The celestials sealed everything they knew at that time via their experiences of the higher worlds and civilizations, such as Lemuria, Atlantis and early Egypt. Yes, they had the ability to view their future life experiences in order to encode certain abilities they would need. However, in their earthly incarnations they would avoid the painful memory that they came from the stars. But at the appropriate time they would awaken to utilize their ability in order to plant seeds that would assist and enhance humanity's consciousness.

To some degree every life does hold a pattern of fated experiences. For example, before reincarnating, your soul evaluates what needs to be accomplished and sets up certain situations and people to be with in that particular life. Some lives are more fated than others, depending on the degree of karma that yet needs to be balanced. Certain experiences do feel more fated than others. Because many of the souls who are awakening have balanced most of their karmic debt, the law of karma is being lifted and replaced by the laws of forgiveness and grace. Grace is a gift that facilitates those who are graduating into the higher energy light in preparation for ascension.

Certain choices during your life journey can free you of your karmic debt. Then, as you no longer have to balance past lifetime experiences, through the law of grace you are free to unveil your spiritual talents in order to serve God and humankind. However, in the beginning you did create your blueprint of purpose to be accomplished from life experience to life experience.

VE: Understood, thank you. Now I would like to know more about that crystal energy force field or band around Earth that seals her inhabitants into so many reincarnation experiences. Why is this needed?

AM: Every realm of existence, whether it is Earth or other planetary systems, all have force shields that will not allow inhabitants entrance into a higher state of being until one can upgrade its energy patterns in order to pass through the force shield's vibratory frequency. It is not the crystal rope force field that imprisons the being, but the being itself who makes the choice to experience duality, emotion, and feeling. The entity itself creates its own imprisonment. The force shields are for protection, because if you are not advanced enough to go through the shields of light, the experience would be very painful. You would get a brief realization of all you had not yet achieved and feel great emotional pain. The Father/Mother God loves you so much that it wouldn't let you come into that realization or awakened memory.

When you are conceived in the physical world, you are genetically gifted with time barriers so that you do not re-member past or future. This way you can continue in your school of learning and advance through experiences that, in time, will provide the beginnings of an open memory. The opening of some memories are now available for the entire human species as our incoming energies stimulate and in-spire your higher consciousness. That is why the star seeds and star children are now awakening with an incredible thirst to return to the higher dimensions and why the star lights are realizing that they, too, can soon experience systems of life beyond Earth. Your long journey is nearly over, beloved ones.

A wonderful cosmic celebration awaits your return.

And now I wish to describe for you the process by which you may become Ascended Masters by purifying your own consciousness and increasing your devotion to the Creator. This path of mastery and ascension is the one already travelled by many great beings who are now assisting you to reach your own graduation goal. Those who work with spirit nearly always achieve their ascension in a much-accelerated way, and the opportunity for graduation in these times is definitely accelerated.

> If you believed that your negative thoughts and emotions were keeping you from becoming an Ascended Master, would you be willing to make some necessary changes?

Chapter 9

The Seven Worlds of Graduation

Throughout the Universe there are multiple dimensions beyond dimensions that humankind cannot presently begin to comprehend. However, let me share a few thoughts about your own Milky Way galaxy for the purpose of giving you some clarity and inspiration. There are many angelic realms that are in service to the Great One, or what you term God. In the beginning, before the worlds of matter existed, the Great One began to dispense the blue flames of purity from the Central Throne to go out and create universes and multiple worlds within worlds. Your planet is part of this process, of course, and has unique features we wish you to understand.

Although you think of the Earth as a solid mass, it is filled with numerous energy portals that can be seen and used when Earth's inhabitants raise their consciousness to a high vibration of light. Not everyone will be able to enter through the same gateways or portals, however, because their frequencies are not at the same spiritual level. The vibrational level of these portals gets higher or more subtle as you progress in spirituality and achieve higher consciousness destinations. There are seven major worlds or levels of consciousness in the soul's journey and humanity begins at your three-dimensional level advancing upward to the seventh. When you reach the seventh level you will have achieved your goal of graduation from this Universe! In case you wonder what the various levels are like, let me now share information about the seven worlds of humanity's graduation process.

As we create the many worlds and dimensions, we appoint both an executive and an assembly of universal agents within each place. These agents are known to you as the angelic servants of light who overview all inhabitants of each region within these created worlds. These angelic beings have different levels of appointments in which each serves somewhere in the higher realms of creation. For the human species to achieve true spiritual consciousness in their particular worlds and hold service appointments in their higher realms there are seven primary competency levels to master or become.

In giving you this analogy concerning humanity's required seven levels of graduation, please understand that each level contains multiple sub-dimensions before ascension from the Universe can be achieved. And then, in the eternity of existence, how new levels are available so you can begin again in another terrestrial sphere of creation. And another. And another. **(See Illustration #13, next page)**

WORLD ONE – THE PHYSICAL BODY

A physical body is needed when the soul chooses to take on a human experience by enveloping itself in matter through the element of carbon. In the carbon state the physical body is itself a living entity or world. We call this body "the living temple of man." This body will learn through the physical states of expression, experiment and experience. *Every thought and action from the personality will be manifested into the cellular level of the physical body.* This world is the hardest world to release because of the memories that attach themselves to the physical body throughout the various experiences of many lifetimes.

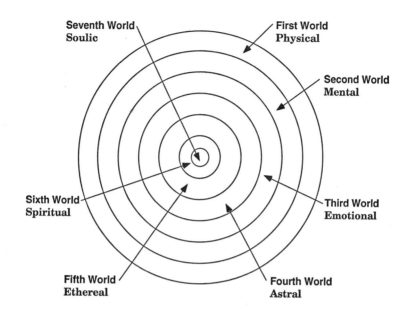

Seventh World
Soulic

First World
Physical

Second World
Mental

Sixth World
Spiritual

Third World
Emotional

Fifth World
Ethereal

Fourth World
Astral

Illustration #13 - Seven Worlds of Graduation

The physical body contains all the living cells of present life actions, previous lives, and the knowledge of your future within its tremendous volumes of information. However, *your past and future experiences are blocked or sealed within the DNA/RNA coding system at conception.*

As humans evolve and begin to release old belief patterns, it's easier to make the necessary changes that the personhood needs in order to grow and unveil the soul's inner truth. Always remember that a state of negative thought or belief will keep that energy imprisoned until it's released into a more loving energy vibration. One way in which the body can release negative energy is when it experiences pain that can no longer be ignored. This pain is actually just buried debris of unmanaged thought that must be recognized and brought into balance. Therefore, through the physical body, the soul is asking the personality to awaken to the cause of the body's pain. It is using pain to stimulate attention and create changes that will eventually allow movement onto a higher state of evolved awareness.

Hopefully, the personality or ego will begin to feel the pain and bodily struggles as challenges, or stepping-stones, in order to initiate a purging or a cleansing of the old ways. Be assured that over eons of experience the physical body will elevate to the higher, physical-etheric body of the fifth world. At that ascension time, the first world physical body accelerates from dense physical to physical-etheric where the cells no longer hold the same memories or patterns of density and where the physical body actually changes its cellular level to a molecular level.

WORLD TWO – THE MENTAL BODY

The second world of the human experience is the mental body that holds the intellectual aspects of lower thought, but will gradually expand into unlimitedness. Until humans can succeed in these broader aspirations, however, they will be caught in the web of intellectual egotism caused by the various negative stages of personality and societal influences. The mental body of thought is the director of its own creation so the adage: "What you think is what you become" is true. *The keys of mastery are power, mind and will.* In time you will learn that you hold the power of the trinity within you.

In the physical world the process of learning through time experiences can expand your mind beyond the limitation of the physical environment. You will have to go beyond how you view your physical world, and raise your thoughts to higher spiritual concepts, which will give you the assistance to overcome physical limitations. Transcending the intellect and connecting to cosmic mind by using the keys of universal wisdom will open your power to achieve self-mastery. This will enable humans to lift their intellect into cosmic mind and unveil the higher states of developed abilities.

WORLD THREE – THE EMOTIONAL BODY

The third world is the emotional body. Emotion means energy in motion or action. The emotional world is very powerful, and it is the primary reason the souls now on Earth chose this particular school to experience. Why? Because this is the embodiment that affords you the availability to touch and feel. The emotional embodiment will react to everything that your thinking produces. So, in time, after many Earth experiences you will realize that you are caught in the three-dimensional school of emotional activity. You will begin to understand that there is choice and that you can choose to be emotionally happy or emotionally sad.

Time itself is the key in realizing that everything experienced through the door of emotion is very temporary. There is never anything that is permanent upon the Earth because all experiences will eventually pass. You experience fleeting moments of happiness such as the birth of a child, meeting your life mate, being recognized as a valued person or even just celebrating a birthday or anniversary. During such times your heart may pound as the emotions produce a brief experience or moment of what you call happiness. However, real happiness is finding a balance within the self so that the connection of tranquility and grandeur can both be realized. Then you can maintain a balance and pull both worlds together, combining the world you truly are with the world that you are living in. When this connection is found, the balance is perfection, and the joy you experience is not fleeting but steady.

At this fulcrum point the emotional body will have lifted up beyond uncontrollable feeling into a state of unconditional love where it can hold a certain quality of truth and bliss. This does not mean that you won't still have fleeting moments of emotion, but you will no longer react in the same manner as before. When you have interlaced with the higher heavenly energies, this world's attachments will no longer hold the same importance for you. The body's emotional world will eventually no longer react to those things that the physical world holds in the illusionary form of duality. In time and with practice, the emotional body will have graduated beyond duality back to the center of oneness. To graduate from this third world, you must expand beyond mere emotionalism and you must be lifted into the universal key of unconditional love.

WORLD FOUR – THE ASTRAL

The fourth world is the doorway that Earth souls go through when they have shed their physical bodies in death. However, there is no death of consciousness, so each soul merely sheds its cloak to be taken to another sphere called the astral world. In this state of being there are many teachers, guides, mentors and angelic servants awaiting the ethereal light body's arrival, ready to assist the soul with further growth. There are vast differences in vibrational frequency within the astral planes of existence and you will need to master many of these dominions in order to graduate to a higher form of your spiritual self. There are thirteen major levels or dominions within the astral world, with each one further subdivided into many other realms, so the astral world is a critical junction to the higher worlds.

Persons from Earth who are not yet awakened, and are choosing the experience of lower nature or darkness, occupy the lower astral levels. They have chosen to reduce their consciousness through the action of a major deed that causes pain or suffering to another. The list of negative behaviors is long—whether personal or national. Creating war for one's personal gratification or holding power over a country to harm its inhabitants and other people are loveless actions recognized by most people. Those responsible for such actions will not be taken to a place of light. Instead, darkness will be their home for a time, because what they chose to create through their thoughts and actions must eventually be experienced. However, there are many different levels of darkness, just as there are many levels of light. So again, the degree of darkness or light to be experienced will be based on the life actions. What may appear as judgment by the celestials is not judgment at all. Rather, the free will choice made by the person has drawn them to the compatible level of energy appropriate for their state of consciousness.

There are angelic guardians throughout the astral levels who show each being, after physical death, the mirror of their soul's perfection so they can immediately see what they have or have not done. This learning process has been called karma or the law of cause and effect. This earthly aspect of the soul will need to address these issues and be placed in one of the various levels of assigned learning. Eventually the soul will acquire another womb and create another blueprint for continuing its lessons on Earth.

Even though it may not appear to be fair or equal, if one looks through the events of their karma account—it is. It may seem that action and reaction or cause and effect are the only eraser through time, but those who embrace the reality of God can also release their karma through love and forgiveness and grace. Everything that is experienced through your life is always in divine right order.

However, please understand that not all experiences a soul chooses are related to a negative karmic pattern. Some souls will simply choose certain experiences because it is for the soul's future purpose to go through these particular things. For instance, if someone is born blind, it could be a karmic situation being brought to balance. Or it may be the soul's choice to fulfill this role in order to prepare itself to work with the blind in a future occurrence. On Earth, experience is generally the only teacher through which one can gain the ultimate wisdom about a condition or situation—and actually become that wisdom personified.

As you continue your soul journey through the doors of death, you do ultimately graduate to higher planes of loving existence in the light. In the higher levels of the astral dimensions you are met by the angelic forces who will take you where you next need to be in the various temples of learning. Over time, all souls are given another chance to look through the mirror of their life, to create another blueprint, and return to continue their life cycle upon the Earth school.

More and more of the physical aspects of souls on Earth

today are feeling that they do not want to come back to Earth. In prayers and meditations we hear you say—"Father, I want to come home. I don't want to come back to Earth again; please let this be my last time here." Those who are awakening and who remember that they come from a far greater place often make these comments. For them, the attachments to Earth seem to be falling away.

This can be the last Earth experience for some people whether they are lifted up through the doorways of death or instantaneously ascend with their physical bodies through the tunnels or shafts of light. These gateways of paradise will open for those who are vibrationally ready and they will be allowed to enter into the ethereal fifth world, another vibration closer to love and light.

There are souls presently on Earth who have already mastered all astral levels by completing the Earth school experiences and shedding the veil of illusion. They now know that they are co-creators with their Creator, have accepted the God Spark within them, and have chosen not to live in separation from the Divine any longer.

In waking up, beloved ones, you realize that you are not from the Earth plane, but are spiritual souls in a human body learning to transcend the illusionary holds of Earth's entrapments and negative thought forms. Duality is the force perpetrated by the Prince of Earth, Lucifer, who creates the illusion of your being separated from the oneness of God. Humanity is not separated from God! God is constant. It is not God who has abandoned humanity, but humanity who has abandoned God. Please remember that God is forever ready to bring that part of itself, which it once gifted you, back into its grace of being.

WORLD FIVE – THE ETHEREAL

The fifth world is the ethereal world, or a world of light, often called the etheric plane. It is the place where souls from Earth who have completed their astral learning have ascended into a physical-etheric light body. There are many of these etheric dimensions found within the hidden doorways of your Universe that cannot yet be seen or fathomed. Be therefore assured that there are many planets, star systems, and galaxies that have life beyond the physical plane, as you understand it.

Mother Earth is also planning to ascend just as you souls are preparing to do. That is why she is spinning in such a high velocity at this time, soon to reposition herself and join the higher systems of light. Please appreciate that within your solar system, Earth is located in the third orbital position, but in time it will raise to the twelfth orbital position because of the blue transmuting flame I am now bringing into Earth. Generally unbeknownst to your scientists, your solar system has twelve planets, three of which are on the other side of your Sun and can't yet be seen, although some astronomers and scientists are exploring this idea. One of these planets is called Michael and is currently located in the twelfth position. However, when Earth's ascension takes place, Michael will transfer to another position beyond this Universe and Earth will take its place.

Then, another existing planet like Earth will be positioned to take the place of your current Earth world. So when the ascension of Earth takes place, the enlightened inhabitants on Earth will also ascend simultaneously. There will be quite a miraculous display of harmonic sounds in the rearranging of all worlds as many angels and Legions of Light gather to welcome those who have come through the gateways. *Please do not confuse this ascension with a present concept among some of humanity that suggests people will be lifted up by space ships.*

It is vital to understand that because other planets and dimensions within your Universe hold a lighter form of matter, the entities within these systems hold a form enmeshed with light particles so their bodies look more transparent. However, they can appear to be human when entering into the frequency range of your Earth system. These beings are highly developed in many of the universal languages of telepathy, whereas you on Earth are the only species who use sound through the vocal chords, instead of utilizing mind transmissions. These beings live in many different dimensions now, over-viewing Earth and helping to assist in her ascent.

The fifth world is the one you on Earth are calling the New Age or the Golden Dawn, and it is a very extraordinary level. *It is unique because when you go through the gateways of light you will meet all the counterparts of your God-self that have simultaneously been existing in other planes of existence. This will be the first time all 144,000 counterparts have been together for 250,000 years.* Peace will reign for a time until another ascension is birthed for those who can again rise to a higher state of spiritual balance. The fifth world is also referred to as the New Expression of Spiritual Discovery.

When you have traveled through the various dimensions of learning in the fifth world you can then go into the sixth world of spiritual consciousness.

WORLD SIX – SPIRITUAL

When a soul has graduated from the world of ethereal light, it is raised to an elevated state for new experiences to be learned in the higher spiritual worlds of unfoldment.

These spiritual realms are the habitat of souls who have the ability to connect into the greater universes and the higher stations of creation. Here, many will choose to come into their collective thought units, as group committees, assisting in the over-viewing of many stations of life and still having the greater tabernacles of assignments. The souls continue to learn and to reach for states of purposeful perfection with spirit. These realms of expertise will allow souls to encounter many higher worlds, working in accordance with the technical matrix systems that interconnect with the interlaced universal communication systems. In the spiritual realm one must advance to an even higher state of universal language than what you understand as telepathy. It is called a mind pictograph language.

Telepathy is the ability to transmit or receive the mental

thought process through units of color, light and sound. But mind pictography is an advanced form of language where the mind has now developed the ability to expand, transmit, and receive images far beyond the individual or group thought projection. By now the soul has learned, through the various stages of growth, to envision the thought waves of everyone throughout an entire planet instantaneously. Some of these beings even have the capabilities to document and record the group mind endeavors, activities, actions and development within a particular star system or planet.

In the sixth world you learn to use the higher advanced states of mind and interlace with various systems to help raise the vibrations of the lower worlds—and create additional spheres to be readied for occupancy for the next graduation from the fifth world. Furthermore, during the sixth world there will also be another gathering of your 144,000 counterparts to ascend once more.

WORLD SEVEN – THE SOULIC

The soulic worlds are highly advanced, and many of these great ones are the overseers of your Universe as a whole. These souls have the attributes of higher law and order assisting in the creating of even greater worlds. The soulic worlds are beyond your planetary systems, star systems of light, and require an executive who is assisted by a multiple level assembly of angelic forces. There are those assigned to these responsibilities who also need many teachers and mentors to assist them.

Each of the seven worlds has its own mode of travel, and the higher the world's vibration, the more sophisticated the techniques are for entering and exiting time, timelessness, energy grids, and the orbital patterns of space. All worlds have their governmental controllers, representatives of light, environmental administrators, timekeepers, record keepers, space patrollers, scientists, and energy equators, ad infinitum.

The soulic world embraces the last dimension that the soul

has to pass through before it can break through the energy force shield. In penetrating this force shield, it allows one to move to a higher expression of one's God-self. In this awakened state of spirit the soul can once again rejoin its counterparts who have coexisted simultaneously throughout life's many sojourns. Now they will collectively experience another ascension that will spiral them out of this Universe they have so diligently and devotedly traversed!

At this point, let me pause and ask for your questions, Virginia.

* * *

VE: Greetings from all of us here and thank you for this clarification. It is sobering to realize that every thought and action we have is manifested into the cellular level of our physical bodies! Please evaluate our current techniques for healing the negative memories in our cells and suggest what other processes would be beneficial. Explain how the body can go from a cellular to a molecular state either before or after physical death.

AM: The most important ingredient for healing negative cell memories is to be awake enough to realize when a negative thought has surfaced, so that you can transmute it by honoring why it is there. Having the ability to recognize a negative thought as it is happening is the first step. Then feel how your emotions are playing out, what they are portraying to you. Is there sadness, grief, anger, aloneness, and so on? Also, see if it is causing a symptom in a particular part of your physical body. Then mentally send light and love to it. Many times when a negative does surface, it's because you have just seen or heard something that has triggered a latent memory. It may be something that you are totally unaware of, or you may be very clear as to what just occurred.

You must look at your own reaction and why you're producing a negative response to the event or situation. Begin to dance with the negative counterpart of you, and see why it has come before you. Don't be fearful. Embrace it and allow it so you can work on transmuting it. To do this, you must take time to meditate and to listen to the inner voice that will give you guidance during this process.

One of the greatest healing tools is the Ha, Ha Mantra. You can sit alone, or in a group and begin in unison saying, "Ha, Ha, Ha, Ha" and keep it going for as long as you can. Memories will surface, as well as visions and feelings.

In doing a group process of the Ha, Ha Mantra, stay in unison and then allow yourselves to rise slowly to higher octaves until you are all laughing out loud. Some will continue laughing until they feel extraordinarily wonderful, and others will succumb to crying. Regardless, it is a tremendous release of your everyday cares and stresses.

The Ha, Ha Mantra works because the "H" has the four L's within it, and through mathematics it holds the number 8 which means "As above, so below." So the H connects you through the process of divine breath to the physical, mental, and emotional body, and then it unites with your higher light body. The "A" means action, so through the HA you are bridging to the source of light within you.

When you release tension through laughter it creates physical, emotional, and mental balance. Laughter will bring energy to higher patterns of light that afford you the opportunity to raise your vibration and emit higher knowledge. Laughter releases endorphins, neurotransmitters and decreases the levels of stress hormones, such as adrenaline. Remember, "He who laughs...lasts!" In your homes and centers you should have daily laughing sessions.

Changes from the cellular body to a molecular one are being done as you take each breath. When you maintain a positive attitude, the kundalini rises, and keeps rising. When all the chakras are in a constant harmonious momentum, your cellular body can begin changing and you can connect to the frequency of the molecular range. Not many on Earth can attain this change at this time. However, there will be those who will achieve this state during the process of ascension, and the molecular state will occur instantly.

VE: How many Ascended Masters have individually graduated through the seven worlds already? Will there be many more individual graduations or primarily a group ascension now? And can you confirm that one million Hathors ascended as a group?

AM: It would be impossible to give you an exact number of how many Ascended Masters have graduated throughout the Earth plane. There have been singular graduations, such as that of Jesus, Gandhi, Mohammed, Buddha, and many others for a long time. *Now the good news is that there is a group that is graduating as a collective group consciousness. This hasn't happened for eons of time!* After this ascension to the fifth dimension, Earth will begin to house her inhabitants to go through the school of duality again. Both singular graduations and another great group ascension will then be offered.

As to your question regarding the Hathors—yes, they did ascend as a group consciousness and are connected to the higher levels of the evolutionary frequency that are at this time assisting humanity. They are giving much assistance via voice, tones, instruments, music, bells and gongs, to help in upgrading the consciousness through the use of energy frequencies of sound and the interceptor chords of harmony.

VE: What are the mechanics required to move Earth from her present orbit to the twelfth planet's position behind the Sun? And to move planet Michael to another Universe? Also, there is a respected writer who says the twelfth planet has uncaring people who have abused Earth and humanity on their infrequent orbital interfaces with us. Is this true? What are the three planets behind the Sun we haven't identified? And do they influence us at all?

AM: The science of rearranging matter and motion into any orbital pattern of holding a higher level of frequency is done by using the powerful units of particles of the Sun to induce an elevated energy shift. When the time is correct we will move all systems throughout the universes into a sequential formation of graduated change.

Graduating Earth to a twelfth position is a way for me to give you an understanding of the extreme shift that Earth herself is going to make. When you think that Earth is going from a third orbital position to the twelfth, that is quite an amazing acceleration.

There are three more planets on the other side of the Sun, which I have used for you to understand that everything pulsates through the vibration of the numeral 12. The 13th will be the doorway/portal that opens for the planet Michael to spin into a higher vibratory rate into another universe. Please keep in mind there is no way humans can presently think in our terms of graduated processes—such as the elements that must come together to rearrange the planets' orbital patterns, or how the spatial time warps and portals are used.

Vega, Lucifer and Michael are on the other side of your Sun, but there are also multiples of 12 x12 x 12 still representing the 144,000 numeric base. You now know of your immediate 12 planets within your system, but there are also numerous planets that equate to the twelfth position throughout your Universe.

The man you speak of as a respected writer is also correct, but his twelfth plane of existence is not the same as I am referring to as the Michael system. I know your minds take everything about numbers in exactness but in reality planetary systems, including your own, cross connect and parallel other systems, planets, galaxies, solar systems and universes.

Please use my analogy about Earth experiencing an incredible energy shift into a higher dominion of accelerated light. Earth will be lifted by the transmutable flame of the Central Sun and enter another world of enhanced light by removing the barriers of a restricted energy frequency. These portals are opened by a suction effect that will in turn produce a whirlwind energy cone that creates a propulsion effect, and this will thrust the energy vibratory rate of Earth into an accelerated higher vibration. This will instantly cause it to be repositioned into a new dimension of consciousness. Remember that another Earth will be ready to take its place.

These words of mine cannot express the thrilling cycle humanity is entering regarding the graduation and ascension process that leads to higher consciousness! But if you respond to the joyful feeling our words engender in your heart, you may achieve a heightened level of vitality, hope and peace. These will be welcome attributes in the coming times.

> Would you fearlessly try to overcome your
> challenges if they provided the opportunity
> for you to grow in strength and courage?

Chapter 10

Coming Times

It is vital that I address the hearts and souls of all humanity as you enter this extraordinary time of change—not only for those living within America, but for all nations on planet Earth. As the 21ˢᵗ Century comes into reality, various changes of a political, social, ecological and an economical nature will occur, and to many of you these will seem traumatic and chaotic. However, I caution you not to see it this way. Whenever a new era comes to pass, all of you who exist on the planet must experience these changes in order to create a new way of living. For you, this means an extraordinary era of time when many will uplift to a state of Cosmic Universal Consciousness, during which the human mind will accelerate and learn to utilize the higher etheric laws of knowledge. This is a remarkable opportunity for the souls who are awakening now to demonstrate their self-mastery and self-sovereignty.

Many of you within America and other nations are here from many eons ago. You have come back once again to pioneer positive use of the higher technologies for these coming times. You have come to Earth to use these higher ways of thinking and these technical devices in total spiritual balance to create peace rather than using these devices in a negative way. Although humanity's mind has been greatly limited, there are those of you who will again use your minds to create a higher vibratory pattern in your bodies. This achievement will allow you to accelerate and transcend the limitation of your Earth body and advance into a physical-etheric body when the time is correct.

The changes that have been happening, and will happen, are for the purpose of helping you balance your attitudes within the two polarities of the positive and negative. Since you have free will and choice given to your soul, you must choose which direction you will go during this time on Earth when the predominant nature contains much negativity. This negativity comes from those who want to control, manipulate, and utilize fear tactics through mind programming strategies. Although the Great One gives humanity free choice regarding the direction it will go, from a spiritual point of view, *one cannot control or manipulate another soul.* Freedom gives humans the choice to grow within its own evolving doorway of spiritual progress. Nonetheless, the dominant world leaders at this time do not follow this universal law. These negative leaders practice manipulation for self-gain, and control over the populace in many different nations.

Now is the time of testing for everyone to determine their spiritual commitments. All inhabitants on Earth are, and will be, undergoing various levels of change in the political, financial, ecological and social areas as part of their spiritual process. These changes are designed to call forth the soul purpose and return humanity back to God. All people are undergoing an acceleration of the mind and the necessity of changing their attitudes. Humanity must turn itself back toward the Creator or be delayed in advancement.

There are too few individuals in the highest office of all governments—be they members of parliaments, legislators, congressional representatives, senators, judicial or civil offices—who are not now entrapped in uncaring principles and activities. The majority of leaders have succumbed to the seduction of money and power. There are a few blessed leaders who will not succumb to these lower desires, because they do care and are earnest in their endeavors to stand for a noble cause or principle. Yet even those with high integrity, when outnumbered, may grow weary in their endeavors. It is regrettable that law, for many, has become the dark side of justice.

When turmoil exists in the populace of cities or nations, whether it is one individual or a group, that chaos can be used for the positive result of turning each person toward spiritual endeavors. It is an opportunity to drop prejudices and self-importance and begin to see each other in love and oneness. This coming time of purification on Earth provides a magnitude of tests to release the behavior of greed, control and negativities.

POLITICAL POWER

There is a group of powerful people in your world who basically control the major decisions of your planet. They only represent 2% of the population, but they control all political, industrial, and financial institutes; most natural resources; the monopolies of corporations, including most major communication systems in broadcasting, television, satellites, and computers; and most civil and judicial systems that maintain the law. This is simply to say that a few rich and powerful individuals control most countries and people through financial manipulation. These loveless ones, whom I call the "central manipulators," hold the major resources of most countries in order to control their financial empires. These people do not care about humanity, except those they can use for their own self-gain. Their ultimate goal is controlling and enforcing their will upon the entire planet. Even as we speak, they are researching and exploring the establishment of other colonies in this solar system.

I remind you again to be alert and awake to the central manipulators, to the one world committee's advancing power to create a global governing system on planet Earth. In this way, the central manipulators would be able to control all people throughout your world, especially those they consider problematic or difficult—which would encompass the larger sections of population. History proves that the majority of people can be controlled through their emotional desires and materialistic cravings. These loveless beings are placing great effort into taking away your personal privacy through the vast power of the supreme computer system that now exists in your world. It has the capacity of electronically tracing everything you do.

MAJOR COMPUTERS

As you know, long ago during the civilizations of Maldek and Atlantis, many beings misused the power of the fire crystals. These same beings are here again because of their karmic patterns and the need to balance their prior erroneous actions. Because of free will, however, they may choose to serve the light or not, as they wish.

Those of you who believe in the light must realize that unless you claim your power as citizens and confront this group's negativity, you are allowing negativity and control to expand into greater darkness. I must emphasize that there are major computers, and their inter-linking programs, now being designed to take away your privacy and freedom.

Just as you have many sophisticated military devices of destruction and acts of physical terrorism there is also a recent development using non-physical terrorists called cyber-terrorists. These cyber-terrorists are highly intelligent humans who have the ability to break computer codes not only for personal monetary gain, but for control of the world's major water, food, utility, communications and financial systems, as terrorist acts. In your future, these computer geniuses could cause major disasters or disturbances that would affect a large population. It is unfortunate that many of these intelligent beings aren't spiritually evolved in their utilization of computer technology. Very few humans are ready for this level of civilization's sudden advancement into higher kinds of technology, which is why it can be misused. If it is not appropriately harnessed with ethical values, then those with superior computer knowledge can create some devastating disasters.

FINANCIAL MANIPULATION

That 2% of humanity that I have previously called the central manipulators of your world are busy controlling the major integrated bank institutions interlaced among all nations. Through these superior computer capabilities, they eventually want to have major terminals that will control records of all input and output of monies through all countries, even countries that have previously held private banking accounts.

The banking institutions have become the controllers of finances through the use of electronic tracers such as ATM, credit and debit cards. Now to cash a check you may soon need both official identification and fingerprinting to avoid fraud. What actually is happening is the financial manipulators are taking you from a cash system to a cashless system that they control. Since most corporations and businesses have become part of the cashless card system, cash is hardly accepted anymore for financial payments. Have you noticed? Have you even been grateful for the change and liked the convenience of cards rather than cash?

In time there will likely be one activated card that will hold all personal information including passports, work history, medical and dental records, vocational capabilities, and all financial transactions. The danger of this trend must be obvious because there is already a plan regarding the implantation of identification chips into animal necks and human foreheads and hands. We have also seen the development of voice recognition and iris scanning. Although this may be presented as a positive protection for you—given the misadventures on Maldek, Mars, and Atlantis, the potential for controlling whole societies is nearer than you think. Thus citizens of every land must stand forth for their freedoms, because freedom is needed for spiritual self-mastery.

Another way the manipulators control people is to both create and benefit from fear and chaos. These central manipulators, who desire to rearrange the economic system of the world, will take full advantage of every opportunity to expand their control over all aspects of human life. Think for a moment about your own security needs such as earning money to provide shelter, water, food, and other necessities, and how they could be affected by a computer or utility crisis.

The most important key to use, at this time, is one of common sense rather than fear. For instance, since some commercial systems you rely on could be affected by any of a number of world crises, wouldn't it be prudent to have a month's supply of water, food, and other normal necessities? In that way, you will have planned for your own needs. I am not saying to horde food and water, but you should prepare yourself and your family for those intervals of breakdown that could occur. *Preparation provides a sense of security, so prepare and* DO NOT FEAR. The influence of fear is what will cause unfavorable shortages and chain reactions in the increased prices of many products.

Whatever your experience, remember that as a soul you chose to be in your particular area to experience whatever happened, just as others must do. Many of the light workers will experience just a few problems and others practically none at all depending on their mental and emotional purity. Regardless of where you live on the planet, the people have all incarnated to experience these times of change in order to shift into their higher consciousness.

Then trust in the reservoir of life, which is the eternal breath within you that guides and directs your existence and experience in the 21st Century. Changes will come and negative events could occur, but no one must despair and give up hope, even though there will be times when many will feel so inclined.

The angels and masters of the higher worlds are always with you and will assist in your process of overcoming challenges and negativity. Because this is your moment to learn to use the gift of *divine discernment*, go within and listen to the infinite voice, for it is the only voice that will give you the wisest guidance for every need. Remember that challenges are steps in the development of inner listening and to the awakening of your divine self—just as the Christ and others throughout your world have previously done. These lords of light were following their inner guidance during their own challenging times as a model for you on Earth to do the same.

GENETIC CLONING

In previous chapters I have already discussed cloning but because of its importance I include it here again. The cloning to which I shall refer is a negative process of mixing the genetic code of one species with another species that is not in its own kingdom. These kingdoms are: human, animal, plant, mineral, and single cell organisms. Your current experiments such as mixing the genes of pigs (animals) with tomatoes (plants) are harmful because it is consists of crossbreeding two inharmonious DNA codes.

As mentioned, cloning is not a new development, but it is *never* appropriate in two cases: 1. when crossbreeding occurs and 2. when humans are created without the God spark of eternal life. Scientists can decode the genetic system and create a humanoid-type being, but can never create the eternal spark of the breath (spirit) of God. *No one can create a body with divine consciousness other than those who have been privileged to insert the prana or the substance that is understood as breath.* However, the breath about which I speak is far greater than the breath you experience in your physical form. This eternal breath holds within it the key to all life and creativity. This eternal breath or spark actually gives birth to what you on Earth understand as the DNA genetic coding.

What I am explaining is that this creation of life or cloning upon the Earth is a miniscule procedure compared to the other multiple composites of life formulas that are used and known throughout the universes. Nonetheless, be aware that while humanity may acquire the ability to genetically create a body, it would lack the pulsation or spark of eternal life given by God.

MEDICAL SYNDICATE

Because most people do not understand the value and extraordinary intricacies of their physical body, their health may suffer due to poor choices in food and other destructive habits. When they are not responsible for growing their own healthy food, they entrust their lives to those that are the providers. The failure of humanity to eat and live responsibly creates ill health because although your religious teachings have outlined appropriate health behaviors, too few follow them.

Especially today in America, you are tormented by many degenerative diseases that require stringent health support. Many of you have relinquished your personal power with life-threatening results that are costly in both physical suffering and financial loss. Society's answer to these health problems has been to create a monopoly of medical doctors, pharmaceutical companies, hospitals, and others who have organized systems of expensive health care that have partially failed the citizenry. These systems have capitalized on the suffering of those who have fallen ill due to a variety of diseases, maladies, and terminal conditions of various kinds. Whether deliberately or accidentally, the monopoly has not honored its ethical code.

Many of the physicians who practice medicine have forgotten the Hippocratic Oath that commits them to do no harm by the treatments that they administer as healers. Besides the ignorance of some physicians, there are those who deliberately set up unnecessary operations, tests, x-rays, and expensive procedures in order to make money for their own self-gain. In America, the land of the free and a wealthy nation, there are insufficient provisions made for its citizens' health care. Medical corporations, hospitals and pharmaceutical companies control health decisions and are some of the largest financial monopolies in your world today. You must ask yourself and your representatives what ethical codes are used by pharmaceutical and insurance companies.

The horrific costs of pharmaceutical drugs that impact both individuals and the nation, are causing declining care, patients' pain and financial hardship. Therefore, much personal suffering and financial worry exist among the people in America, and in many other countries as well.

Since insurance groups are run for profit they institute regulations to assure financial gain. This means that some people cannot have adequate treatment if they are only covered by for-profit insurance companies.

These insurance regulations generally stipulate that alternative or holistic treatments are not covered at all. Furthermore, insurance companies often won't insure doctors who use holistic healing, herbology, radionics, magnetic healing, imagery healing, crystal healing, sound and tone healing and many other fields. Some are beginning to cover alternative treatments such as acupuncture, chiropractic care, homeopathy, and hypnosis. The major issue that looms before technological societies is prevention through a healing life style that uses more natural healing substances and techniques offered by alternative health practices.

The right to privacy is one of the most cherished freedoms that humans can have, and at this time on Earth it is being taken away in many walks of life. Your right to privacy regarding your medical records is an important issue because they are now being distributed into massive data bases. Drug companies, hospitals, insurance companies, and some employers seek to secure medical information regarding genetic history and previous illnesses in order to avoid the costs of providing adequate treatment.

I really want to honor the many wonderful physicians who do have compassion and who truly do want to help the people. You are fortunate that some doctors now want out of these rigid controls, and are establishing their own healing centers where they may be free to diagnose and choose the appropriate course of treatments and payment.

As you can observe, the medical manipulators do not want people to have freedom to choose the Earth's natural healing agents, which cannot be patented. Vitamins, herbs and organic foods have healing properties appropriate for good health and for prevention of degenerative diseases. Because products in health stores are becoming a booming business, traditional medicine is now attempting to legally control what can be sold in health stores without prescriptions. As people separate from the usual medical establishment's control, more holistic ways of healing will grow as a solution to the degenerative diseases now running rampant. It is to be hoped that costs of vitamins, herbs, homeopathic remedies, other supplements and alternative methods will not become another materialistic manipulation of the sick and poor.

ATOMIC POWER

In the same way your scientists have misused genetic cloning, they have also played God by misusing atomic and hydrogen power for military purposes. By understanding the power of the Sun and splitting the atoms for destructive purposes, they began a free will choice to interfere with the natural processes of creation. Many governments have continued in the testing and detonation of atomic and hydrogen weapons. Bombs exist in most countries of your Earth, and missiles have been strategically placed in order to form a weapon arsenal for both protection and attacking other nations. Atomic and hydrogen testing has continued above and below ground, causing an incredible imbalance within the Earth's structure.

The ocean floors are beginning to crack, and ocean waters are rising at an advanced rate. Some of the nuclear testing caused a heat sweep (volcanic disturbance), and now there is a great melting of your icebergs. *Water is a critical issue.* I assure you that the released radiation from many sources has caused serious problems throughout the Earth on many levels. The atomic misuses by those who have been in power are causing upheavals in your Earth's atmosphere, are causing the Earth to shift, and are creating a terrible devastation on human lives through the political games of war.

Furthermore, nuclear power plant failures such as the horror of Chernoble also take their toll. Such accidents are more common than you think. You may wonder what is worse—atomic accidents or the excessive toxic wastes now being buried as land fill or dumped in your oceans. Please remember, it was through Maldek's misuse of very sophisticated weapons based on fire crystals—an energy of the Sun—that they eventually destroyed themselves. The question you must answer is—are humans headed towards a Maldekian catastrophe? If so, what is *my* responsibility as a light worker?

BIOLOGICAL WARFARE & CHEMICAL TIME BOMBS

The scientists on Earth have also begun to experiment with deadly toxins, viruses, nerve gas, and other dangerous substances that have been created. Although Americans view other nations as the potential threat in the use of these weapons, there are military secrets you know little about. These many substances that scientists have created, and are still experimenting with, are designed to wipe out not just the military, but the general population and even humanity's food and water supply. The military is in the developmental stages of even greater mechanisms of disaster.

I truly urge you to be aware of what your government, scientists, and military services are doing and I implore those who are the creators of biological and chemical horrors to desist from these activities. Human law, government, and political actions are either supportive or non-supportive to human life and spiritual integrity.

COSMIC AWAKENING

Finally, I want to conclude with some thoughts about many of the changes that have occurred and will be occurring because of those loveless ones who are utilizing technology destructively to immobilize and imprison humanity. As mentioned, the computer technology is interfacing with all the government systems not only throughout America, but also with many other nations. I am speaking only of the key countries that are working as world bank systems and that are collectively interconnected in order to become a committee to control the world. There are those humans in positions of power who have the ability to control many Earth conditions such as your weather, Earth shifts, oceans, and even the events of vandalism in your heavens, with their sophisticated instruments.

Speaking of your heavens, I want to briefly mention the solar flares that are causing many shifts upon your planet. These flares are charged with solar particles that affect Earth's magnetic fields, and also your physical, mental and emotional bodies. Many people are beginning to feel more irritated, disoriented, and are even having minor lapses of memory, confusion and frustration. These solar flares are causing your Earth's upper atmosphere to expand through the intensity of heat and that expansion is affecting many areas of your Earth's communication systems.

In addition, there are those within your military who are working on what you term the HAARP program, which will also cause great stress to your upper atmosphere by using the electro-magnetic fields that cause heat waves of dispersed laser beams to be directed there. The electro-magnetic beams work like a boomerang returning back to Earth and causing many levels of damage to both the Earth's grids, and to human beings. There are many other projects presently underway that are ready to be instigated into your everyday lives, which could be quite harmful. However, *what you don't see in the midst of all this negativity is that there is a Divine Intervention occurring and you are part of that intervention. That is the good news and the hope for humanity!*

What do I mean by a Divine Intervention? There are those of you enlightened beings on Earth who have many gifts of spirit and multiple levels of knowledge that can once again be used as your future becomes more apparent. For example, there are some highly skilled computer scientists who are awakening to their psychokinetic abilities and telepathic power, and who will be assisting in new ways of defense against the intrusion into personal lives and records. Some will utilize their remote viewing ability to look into various geographical locations and see any secret negative activities. There are even those who will have the ability to uplift their physical body vibratory rate so high that they will not be seen or heard as they pass through various locations of importance.

As a part of this process *it is vital for you to begin to pay more attention to the time shifts and time expansions you experience.* For instance, there are occasions when you are driving your car somewhere that should have taken about an hour to reach your destination. However, to your dismay it took you three hours. You wonder what happened. This time shift can also work in reverse so that a destination which should take several hours to reach, actually only takes 30 minutes! Sometime you may be driving within an area that you are definitely familiar with, but all of a sudden you become disoriented. Nothing looks familiar. You can't seem to get your bearings; you may feel your heart begin to beat rapidly. If this happens you are probably experiencing a momentary vibrational time shift from which you will suddenly come back to everyday consciousness and instantly be aware of your surroundings again.

What I am suggesting, beloved ones, is that as you now receive the higher physical-etheric energies around you and the planet, you will have more altered states of consciousness that hold unusual powers. However, they need to be balanced and used constructively. To aid humanity's progress you will increasingly be more connected to your guardians, angelic councils and Earth's Inner World masters from whom you will receive extensive knowledge that will be needed in these greater times.

The gifts that you hold are many, but you have forgotten

these ancient technologies that are so sophisticated they surpass what is already being used on Earth today. Because there are many systems of psychotronic weaponry being designed, experimented with, and used in some of the countries of your world, we are deeply concerned. Therefore we are supporting those of you who are willing to develop your mind power to ward off these negative psychotronic thoughts. This mind power development is called mind radionics. Through your development, you can protect each other and the various centers doing light work.

There will also be other humans re-awakening in non-technical fields who will utilize the higher rhythms of mind energy to instantaneously heal themselves and others, to counsel those in need, and help educate many people. They will bring forth art, literature, music, and joys of the soul.

Remember that this is one of the most magnificent times to be on Earth, so be awake and aware and know that you will open to your fullest potential exactly at the right time. This is a glorious era to be alive and each soul is growing more excited as it senses the closeness of the new world to be birthed. You have come at this time to awaken and to recreate another Golden Dawn civilization. Enjoy the challenge! Enjoy one another! You are not alone.

And now, would you like to ask any questions, Virginia?

* * *

VE: Once again I send greetings to you and offer gratitude for the information you share even when it is difficult to hear. I suspect that this chapter could leave some readers feeling very discouraged because of all the negativities mentioned—especially when you say that the changes are for helping us balance our attitudes about positive and negative polarities—that it's a time of testing. What specific things do we need to accomplish for the divine plan? Do you have any specific recommendations for staying balanced during challenging events?

AM: Know that I come to assist those souls who can be the illuminators, and beacons of light, who will help to pave the way to the new world by being the awakened demonstration of the spiritual self called the Christ. The Christ means pure light and love and is the personification of Oneness. I do not come to deliver negativity or to stir up fear. *I come to teach you how to transmute fear, but in order to transmute it you must know how it works and how to recognize darkness. Only when you know what is happening in your world can you neutralize negativity/ darkness.* This does not mean that you have to entertain it or give it energy, but you should be awake enough to neutralize your own fear and maintain balance within yourselves. There are those who want to return home to us, and who realize that the time of changing consciousness is now. I would ask that instead of seeing through the eyes of duality, which keeps you in fear and in the world of illusion, that you see through your God-eye. Then you can see through the disguises, awaken to who and what you are, and comprehend why you have come to participate in these greater times of change.

Remember that you are spiritual beings in a physical form who have the ability to unveil latent talents and to make a genuine difference. Yes, there are tests that your souls set up for yourselves in order to graduate to a higher plane of spiritual consciousness. This testing helps you to understand your world, to stand up for principles that will assist in creating peace, and to aid as many others as you can along the way. Until you neutralize darkness and ascend, you are learning to live in two worlds at the same time—the world of your spiritual self and this physical world.

Currently on Earth there is much darkness because of the rampant negativity that is flooding the minds of people. I am not speaking to those who truly are awakening and who use their compassion and goodness in service to humanity. But there are those who are killing each other in the name of Christ, starting wars in the name of greed, control and the misuse of power. Many people are becoming dehumanized because of the sophistication of computers that label you as a mere number in a system. Many no longer feel connected to each other on a personal level so violence increases.

Some people are watching an actual war on their television as though it were a movie. They are numbing out, becoming unconscious and having very little compassion for the value of those lives being taken. There are others who want even more bombs to be dropped, even more devastation. If it were your country under attack I am sure your perspective would be quite different. There are people all over your world taking the lives of others simply because they don't like the color of their skin or because they hold different belief systems. *This is not the teaching of God!* So yes, there are tests that are being placed before you to help you to wake up and become spiritual beings again.

Those who are awakening will not need these severely challenging tests, but will be protected and guided. My remarks are for those whose hearts are hardened and who simply refuse to turn back to God. For them the spark of their own soul is producing these tests to help them elevate and have a change of heart, even if it is just a miniscule vibration of higher light.

Why are there so many people going through wars, disease, volcanoes, hurricanes, floods, and earthquakes at this time? In one way it is a part of prophecy, but it is also both individual and collective consciousness that have set these tests into motion. For example, during the aftermath of a catastrophic earthquake or flood, no one asks rescuers what their religious beliefs are or notices their ethnic background. No judgment enters into the process as individuals work in unity to pull victims free of debris or from flooding waters. The only common ingredient that is "known" or "felt" in them is the presence of God's love and concern. All humans need to let go of judgment and self-righteousness and lovingly respect and honor each other.

During these challenging times, the grace of God will be with you in accordance to your own divine purpose. It's very simple. You cannot graduate for another, and another cannot graduate for you. However, you can unite and join together in sharing and demonstrating your spiritual talents and your love for all people regardless of their age, gender, race, creed or color.

VE: It is difficult not to judge the loveless beings who commit the worst crimes against humanity and all life. Can you explain why some people are so cruel and don't incarnate on Earth with higher values

AM: I know it is sometimes difficult to understand when there are so many different degrees of soul levels walking upon the Earth at this time. There are young, intermediate, old and master souls all intermingling together, and they all are in their appropriate roles for developing the greater plan.

However, no one can judge another as to the role it plays or what it is choosing to work out in a single life experience. Only the source within the living entity knows of its station in life. Souls have many different incarnations in order to grow and transmute negativity. When an entity begins its journey on Earth, it is like going into a closet where there is only a tiny light bulb and great darkness. Through multiple life experiences, the entity begins to awaken and eventually its light begins to rise to a higher voltage. As the light burns brighter during additional incarnations, the light accelerates into a higher vibration and soon there is no longer darkness. What happened to darkness? Darkness didn't leave. It was the degree and power of the entity's light that neutralized the darkness.

There are many degrees or levels of darkness, just as there are many levels of light. It takes many lifetimes through the astral planes before an entity shifts to light and leaves the dark passages behind. You have all walked through the hallways of darkness but have elevated through the experiences of lifetime after lifetime into a higher consciousness of light. There are those of you who still have to neutralize the petty annoyances of negativity in order to create a stream of light to neutralize all darkness. That is why each of you still faces pockets of negativity that arise within your lives offering you the opportunity to transmute these negative thoughts.

There are tests that a human will set up during its lifetime to see if it really has put aside its old ways of temptation. As another way of balance it may gift its life in order to save or protect another. Regardless of the scenario, please remember that all souls are loved by the Eternal Oneness, and out of that love it allows the entity to choose its own time sequence for advancement into a higher soul expression. There is no one who can cast a stone upon another, for all have erred or are erring. That is why no one can judge another. It is forbidden.

However, if you do encounter an upheaval or have unpleasant experiences, regardless of what occurs, know that it is your soul that has chosen the situation to create a balance regarding something that was left undone. You can either resist or mature through the wisdom of the event. Even though you, the personality, may not understand how it works, the soul does. Everything is in divine right order! So this calls forth an enormous amount of trust and faith in the journey through life.

VE: Your remark that it is only those who have been privileged to insert the prana or substance understood as breath contradicts the belief that God creates humans. Please identify who creates the souls and how they do it.

AM: All souls are created by the breath process of the living source you call God; however, there are many universes and many different levels of creative life forms. As I mentioned earlier, in the beginning God created the Tribunal Godhead which birthed from within itself the seven mystic flames and the twelve eternals who would carry its omnipotence, and the creative patterns of life, to outwardly create physical worlds. Once they had created these worlds, they had to oversee the creative process of life forms within each habitat.

This means that there are a few great beings who are privileged to use the life force code that can assist in the process of creating life. These are known as the Universal Agents who carry the personification of the life force of Oneness and they overview the birth processes that are created throughout all systems of the Universe. Nonetheless, the source you call God is the original and ultimate life-giving breath that exists. Now and always, it will be the only source capable of giving the consciousness of eternal life.

Chapter 11

Ascension and the Spiral of Infinity

In an earlier chapter I explained the seven levels, or worlds, of consciousness, through which humanity must travel for graduation—a goal earned by your own spiritual growth and ethical actions. During daily life on Earth, the word graduation generally means moving higher from one class of study to another until a particular field is perfected or a higher level of qualification is achieved. In that idea of learning and achievement, heaven and Earth are not so different. However, *spiritual graduation is measured by the vibratory frequency of the energy you hold which is different than mere intellectual knowledge.* The important point is that graduation is not the quick act of ascension, but an on-going awakening you must apply each day to perfect yourself by releasing negative thoughts and actions. Only by using the positive inclinations of higher consciousness can you advance through multiple increments of improvement.

As you begin to let go of old beliefs and incorporate the results of the tests that life provides you, then you take responsibility for your own actions and cease to blame others for your life events and lessons. This attitude of responsibility is one way to know that you are graduating out of a limiting set of beliefs into a new way of thinking and living. *Graduation occurs when you can surmount challenges and recognize what you have learned, being grateful for the struggle that motivated you into another new life experience.*

There are many different definitions of mental graduations, but the greatest is when you are able to release old beliefs that have imprisoned you in self-righteousness, judgment and violence toward others. All souls upon this planet from the lowest to the highest will eventually graduate from one level to another. Even if you have no consciousness of light at all but suddenly have brief good thoughts or actions you will have made an initial step upward from that imprisoned unconscious state. All humans, regardless of their stations in life, will have some brief moments of expanded thinking that moves them forward into the greater rays of life. In that expansion, thoughts of inspiration usually find their way into an action or deed.

Humanity must graduate in the understanding that all breath contained in each of your physical bodies—regardless of culture, gender, age, color, race or religion—comes from God. It is humanity with its many false dogmas that keeps you from the divine and eternal love. You have to let go of your loveless or negative thinking and come back to the Source as it breathes its eternal life force through each and every one of you.

So here you are, beloved ones of Earth, in various levels of the graduation process. Now you may be wondering how these graduation levels relate to ascension—a current topic of interest among many humans. Ascension occurs when you have gone through the various lessons of love and forgiveness and have been able to break the ties of imprisoned thinking. Then you no longer carry judgment against your fellow beings regardless of your differences. When you can allow each person to be at his or her own level of growth without judgment, you are seeing through your spiritual eyes. Demonstrating your own concern for all life through your daily activities also indicates that you are aware of your divinity and that you want to return home again.

In many of you, now, the ache for home is strong, the motivation is stirring, and the ecstasy of knowing that it is growing closer may bring tears of joy. When you look into the eyes of a tyrant you can wish he could understand the joys that you are now fully experiencing in just being. Even though others don't understand, you can still hold the balance of love within you, knowing that in time everyone will arrive. By being the embodiment that houses the eternal breath and knowing that you are its experience, experiment and expression, you will have opened the paths of light that bring the enlightenment and joys of the higher worlds to Earth.

There are some in times past who have earned their individual ascension because they used the mastery of will and love power to overcome the imprisonment of duality. Think of the great beings who have walked your Earth and have held strong to their convictions of the higher heavens. They would not bend their knees to the will of man. You call each of these persons, who made their ascension by successfully completing their cycle upon Earth, Ascended Masters. These Masters are now working diligently with many of you to help you to maintain strength, courage and will.

Besides this individual graduation process leading to ascension, *it is now time for another great ascension to take place not only upon your Earth, but throughout all the universes. This is not an individual graduation earned by one soul, but is a collective group experience that allows many to leave the three-dimensional Earth plane in simultaneous ascension.* Because of this divine plan excitement is growing throughout the dimensions of the heavens. The joy is overwhelming while we await word from the Great One that the time has come and the wholeness of light will begin to create a multiplicity of new worlds.

This means that I, the Archangel Michael, will gather all my Legions of Light from this Universe to meet with the omniverses throughout time and we will come to gather the souls of your Earth who will be ready to go through the doorway of ascension. Everyone who holds the seal of light in their third eye will rise into a greater world that will only allow the vibration of peace and divine love. These individuals who can raise their vibration by centering within will have the ability to open the sacred portals through telepathic means, and may be able to receive spiritual direction and knowledge for these greater times of change.

Now let me share what the three great doorways of ascension are so you may have a greater understanding of how they apply to you.

ASCENSION THROUGH THE ILLUSION OF DEATH

There are humans now choosing to leave Earth through the doorway of what you experience as physical death. Upon reaching their appropriate spiritual level those who are awakened need not come back to the Earth plane and will be taken to a beautiful place until the final ascension is birthed. They will have many assignments helping their loved ones on Earth to grow and come back into the arms of God in preparation for the final ascension of this Earth.

ASCENSION THROUGH THE PORTALS OF EARTH

There will be a time when Earth's many human inhabitants will fall into greater and greater degrees of darkness. The light beings still on Earth who have diligently demonstrated their divine gifts of peace will *not* have to stay during the final hours of darkness. For them, the portals of time, which are the major vortex entrances, will open throughout the world and the light workers will be taken through the invisible doorways into the Earth's Inner World cities of light. Two people could be side by side and in an instant one will simply disappear because of their higher vibration. Consequently, both individuals and groups will actually disappear as the higher beings allow entrance into the hidden cities of light within your Earth's Inner Worlds. Here, in a loving environment, these dedicated light workers will be welcomed and will remain until the glorious finale.

ASCENSION THROUGH HEAVEN'S DOORWAY

There will eventually be a time when I, the Archangel Michael, will come to gather all beings according to their spiritual vibrations, and those of the light will be taken into their next heavenly home. These individuals will be identified by the light emanating from their auric fields, and they will be able to pass through the brilliance of the living flame. They will be taken into the new city of light to begin another evolutionary opportunity for growth and service. It will be a thrilling and exciting homecoming.

GRADUATION FOR THOSE WHO ARE LEFT

The beings whose auric fields were not bright enough to pass through the filter of holy light, will be returned to the fourth world (astral) level to again be prepared for another bodily incarnation on a new Earth school. Depending on the soul's evolutionary level, each human will be given the appropriate coding of life as it continues its sojourn in three-dimensional experiences of duality. If the soul was close to attaining ascension, it will then come back at another time on Earth to be a teacher of higher philosophy or to serve humanity in an obvious way. The souls who are still without the consciousness of light, will continue to advance through the astral planes of learning until they can individually ascend or participate in another future collective group ascension into the fifth world of light.

Be assured that after this glorious finale, all beings will be repositioned in their appropriate heavenly domains, and some will begin a journey on the new Earth that has graduated to take its glorious position as the twelfth planet in your solar system.

Here, a new existence will start for the souls of the Golden Dawn, New Age or what is known as the Millennium time of peace. Words cannot truly express what this means to you, but your sacred heart and soul are exuberant. If you listen quietly to your inner feelings of reassurance and love, you will feel the touch of hope and spiritual richness.

MICHAEL DESCRIBES LIFE AFTER THE ASCENSION

Come with me in your imagination to see what life after the ascension will be like in order to amplify that touch of hope and spiritual richness for you. Let it be known that during the 21st Century there was a time when Earth graduated to a higher position within the Cosmos and was relocated behind the Sun in the twelfth orbital position in your solar system. The souls who had opened their minds and hearts to the vibration of Oneness went with Earth as physical-etheric beings. These humans who ascended had gone through many incarnations and experiences in order to learn how to awaken to their spiritual identity and overcome the stepping stones of negativity. They had become competent in using their God capabilities through the divine power of love.

History records that the greatest tests on Earth before ascension occurred in the latter days when spiritual mastery required each human to stand strong and stay balanced and loving to everyone—even in the middle of chaos, deprivation, and war. There were many temptations but some persisted in holding onto their devotion to God, which creates peace, and always paves the way to a higher pathway of life. Many communities had been formed which assisted the humans in maintaining their equilibrium and commitment to the light, and sustained them through the rigors of change.

I, the Archangel Michael, had gathered my Legions of Light and had collected everyone among the population who had a flame of light emanating from the middle of their forehead. Through their love, deeds of service, and staying true to God they were readily identified to be lifted into another dimensional vibration of the etheric world of light. When the sign was given they entered the harmonious vibration of the shafts of light that were opened.

The elements of heaven created a vortex of wind that began whirling like a tornado, and this energy tore open the previous force field shield around the Earth's canopy. When the force field was opened the angelic messengers came and covered every part of the planet. Earth was now in the position to ascend, and with a quickening action the angelic forces created a higher velocity so Earth and her light servers who were ready could arise to a higher station.

During this ascension there were some who were allowed to stay within Earth's Inner Worlds to continue their progressive soul path. There were others who ascended into an angelic city called the New Jerusalem where they were taken into another realm of the higher heavens. There were also those who ascended into the solar system's twelfth position on planet Earth to begin the New Millennium or the Golden Dawn.

It was an extraordinary and joyous moment for the star seeds, star lights and star children because their inheritance was now realized. Their bodies were instantly rearranged from physical-dense into a physical-etheric state, which allowed them total recall of their former telepathic language. It was somewhat different for the star lights when they ascended into their physical-etheric bodies because while they immediately awakened to telepathic abilities they had never experienced the other worlds. Consequently they needed to be schooled in the higher efficiencies of thought language.

GIFT OF ASCENSION

When the humans ascended, they were met by many of the Ascended Masters and angelic hosts to help them stabilize and adjust to their new heavenly place. Those who had just attained ascension-hood, were given work appointments as Ascended Masters in the holding stations to help some physical-etheric beings soon to take on human form. They helped them make appropriate decisions about their soul journey because the new Masters had already walked the density of the three-dimensional Earth themselves and had experienced challenges in order to transcend the tests of separation. Some were assigned to certain group souls or individuals on the new Earth to help them through their Earth journey. Of course, there were numerous other ways in which these new

Masters served the greater light throughout the Universe.

Now in the Golden Dawn, there is no longer pain, suffering, or aging, because the physical-etheric bodies remain as youthful as if they were in their 30's. The physical-etheric bodies are strong, energetic, and beautifully perfect. While each individual holds patterns of androgynous characteristics, through the law of nature they choose which form they prefer, either feminine or masculine. There are some beings who choose to hold both genders uniting as a cosmic group working together in unison.

There are no wars, cruelties, brutalities, greed, or misuse of power here, only an overseeing government that is composed of a celestial council who maintain the vibration of Oneness for this ascended planet of light.

From the new Earth's position you look out into the heavens where the sky holds beautiful colors of intricate blues, lavenders and pinks. The sky now has two suns and two moons because both solar and lunar energies are needed for the planet's nurturing process. The new Earth will never experience darkness because it is transparent like a crystal. The cities are crystal-powered, crystal-structured and the light is far greater than any ever experienced on three-dimensional Earth.

This wondrous new planet has many beautiful hills, mountains, oceans, lakes, flowers, animals and even foods, but they are fruits that taste like nectar. Since there is no longer any killing or eating meat these wonderful elixir fluids and fruit-like substances are used to maintain the body for much longer periods of time. Food is primarily used for sustaining life.

RELAXATION TIME

New souls who have just ascended need a period of rest, and during this rest period they are able to create and do those things which they have longed for. This joyful rest and relaxation reward is given immediately, and is somewhat like taking an extended vacation anywhere you want to go. Also,

184

when it passes through the ascension flame, the soul requires a certain time to replenish itself and to be reoriented into its new vibrational surroundings. There are many celestial helpers assigned in order to assist in this transitional period. After this time of rest, teachers begin to prepare the new arrivals for their necessary work appointments as servers of the infinite light at the level of their capabilities and interests.

FAMILY RELATIONSHIPS

There are souls who join together to continue procreating the life of new generations of souls to be birthed into this new world. When two beings come together they can energetically interlace telepathically within the ebb of divine union, which in turn will generate a higher spiritual connection. Through the physical-etheric rhythms of their body, mind, and soul, a light seed is produced. This seed is given to the creative producers until the infant is birthed. Then it is returned to the cosmic parents to be loved and nurtured until it must enter into a school according to its abilities and interests.

SCHOOLS OF LEARNING

The schools of advanced learning are multiple in the Golden Dawn realms. Each being can choose educational interests to further perfect their abilities. For example, the humans who were healers on Earth may choose to continue their development into higher healing knowledge and capabilities. Some may have the ability to travel to other systems of light to advance certain techniques or skills. Also, specific assignments will be offered in giving guidance, delivering messages, healing, nurturing, and even making appearances to those who are in need of a spiritual awakening. The available service areas are numerous, and all beings live for the joyful opportunity to serve others with their spiritual talents.

THE CREDIT POINT SYSTEM

In this particular system of light, there is no longer a monetary system such as humans had once known. Everthing is now done for the pure joy of being in service and continuing to learn in the greater tabernacles of many systems. When someone is appointed an assignment, the individual has a specified time during which the work must be completed, which in turn earns credits, either to be used for relaxation, entertainment, travelling, or developing special interests according to their own choice.

ASCENSION AGAIN

After all of the five levels of consciousness have been attained, a continuation of certain tests assists each being to continue its growth into a greater level of light. These beings will still have the inner motivator that will keep pushing them forward to achieve their greater potential in order to ascend into even higher stations of light.

In a future experience, of course, the tempter will come again with negative thoughts intended to create interference that will disrupt the flow of love and peace. There will be those who will succumb to the misuse of power, who will not want to live in the law of Oneness, which will then start another cycle of negativity. This will begin the challenges to see which beings will remain steadfast and devoted to the Oneness. Those advancing souls will have to rise above the negativity once again in order to ascend from the fifth ethereal world into the sixth world of spirituality.

This negativity will not be the same as humans experienced during their journey of duality on the Earth school, but one that works through the law of nature that also creates challenges in order to pass the greater flame of light. And so the eternal life continues, beloved ones, and you grow in love, wisdom and spiritual consciousness, drawing ever closer to the Great One and the higher celestial dimensions.

Here I will pause, Virginia, and ask what questions you may have.

* * *

VE: Greetings again and enormous gratitude for the good news contained in this chapter. We appreciate the information very much! Please clarify your statement that light workers won't have to stay on Earth during the final days of darkness. Is this when the portals and vortices open? If so, will the light workers have any warning? And does their home location have any significance as to where they'll be directed to go?

AM: I have described three different levels of ascension. One of them will be when the illuminators, or those who will hold the Christ light, will overcome the darkness by awakening to the divine aspect of love. In their goodness, they will acknowledge and love all beings.

Darkness is the negative thought that produces an action such as greed, misuse of power, cruelty, hate and war either by nations or individuals. The illuminators must stay balanced and maintain their light, not succumbing to those emotions. As they maintain their light they will be allowed to ascend into another vibration or plane of existence. Many doorways will be opened, and there will be a time when some can depart from this world. There will not be a warning; it will happen instantly. You will not have to be in any particular location when this occurs because there are ways wherein the portals of each soul will open and instantly shift into a physical-etheric being—no longer maintaining a dense physical vibration. As these doors open, the light servers will pass through immediately. Many guides will be on the other side awaiting their arrival.

However, some of the light servers will choose to stay behind to help during the greatest time of darkness. These souls who remain will be called the "saints of time" for their willingness to pave the way for the greater ascension that is still to come.

Today upon your Earth, darkness/negativity is becoming more predominant and it is easy for one to submit to it out of fear and insecurities. However, the test is: Can you keep your light shining while walking in the midst of darkness, and not fall prey to its influence? To be negative is easy. But to uphold your integrity, stay balanced and continue to love is not an easy task. When you have really connected to the divine within, you have power, strength, and an awakened sense of knowingness, wisdom, and divine justice. With all your heart and with all your might, you will worship only Oneness with transcendent strength and joy.

VE: Although some of the light workers are good at manifesting what they personally want, as a group we can't seem to achieve our heart's desire to manifest a greater state of peace on Earth. Is there something different we need to do? Or is manifesting peace presently beyond our power?

AM: Manifestation comes in many forms, such as material things, spiritual awakening, and manifesting a higher knowing that allows great accomplishments through your gifts and abilities. Achieving in groups will be necessary as you continue forward in your Earth lives, even though many humans are still stuck in the power struggle of their ego. When spiritual centers are built, and humans begin to find their true cosmic families, there will no longer be the same struggles for personal power. Each member will gather together for the betterment of the whole group and for humanity.

To manifest as a group, you must meditate and visualize what you need. Not one person can lose focus and wander in thought. Their mutual intent must be connected in absolute mind unison. Not keeping in unison will distract and disturb the required flow for the act of manifesting. This will take work, but there are groups that are now beginning to have successful experiments with these techniques. Some humans are better at receiving than transmitting; some transmit better than they receive. Others have the ability to do both. You ultimately need experience in both levels of development.

Manifesting peace must come within each soul first and foremost. Then as you gather together you can build the momentum of utilizing your talents and become the demonstrators of peace. There are many who are now gathering together in group consciousness. But in order to create the amplified power, the most important thing is joining the various positive *groups* together as a collective consciousness and not remaining separated.

There will be those of lower nature thinking who will try to distract and deter you, but they can't hold the position for long as they will recoil back from the power of your light. Continue forward, grow stronger, and always know that a sun is rising regardless of how it may appear in the illusion. Don't fall prey to the illusion; stay strong and know that you are manifestors. Trust your unlimited Universe.

VE: For those of us who yearn to experience ascension but aren't sure we can graduate yet as an Ascended Master, can you give us a more thorough explanation and description of the group ascension process?

AM: Gladly! On Earth there are many humans who are diligently working in preparing for what is known as the group ascension. This is purposeful for you in order to elevate to a higher spiritual frequency and pass through the doorways of light to the ethereal worlds. Earth is considered the lower heaven, which has been kept isolated by the crystal rope force shield that restrains Earth and her inhabitants in the lower heaven's frequency. Because of this lower density, you are experiencing separation through the law of duality and the curtains of illusion.

As mentioned, Earth herself is also preparing to ascend by spinning into a higher velocity and will in time be repositioned into a higher heavenly station. Remember that Earth and the astral realms are presently in the lower heaven's vibratory rate, so these realms can not connect to the ethereal/ light realms. The Astral world and its many levels of learning were created as a holding station for humans who passed through the veil of death, and were then reborn into another body. Until one could pass the tests of Earth and ascend to the ethereal or the higher worlds of light, the astral levels were the only possible placement. That is all changing, however, because of the nature of God, which I shall now explain.

The main concept you must grasp about ascension is that the Source is not a static essence with a rigid nature. It did not just birth some life forms and then quit. To the contrary, the

Father/Mother God, as you know it, is forever growing into the greater part of itself. That is why ascensions are so important. Because of them the Source is ready to rebirth itself once again whenever enormous amounts of light return to it. Although there are many singular ascensions that take place throughout the eras of time, long periods must pass before a "supreme" or a large group ascension can occur. This is where life forms from all systems within your Universe and others will collectively be drawn together like a magnet into a force of light.

Soon a supreme ascension will take place throughout your Earth and connect all souls in the Universe who have also elevated in consciousness. You will collectively emerge as a radiant burst of light that creates a fire breath (life force pulsation) that is instantly felt by the center core of the Source. It is then that it instantly rebirths itself by creating new universes and worlds. During a supreme ascension, then, many universes uplift simultaneously. This event is fantastic!

The more souls who can elevate to achieve ascension simultaneously the greater the Source can expand beyond its moment in time to create greater spirals of infinity. The splendor of the Creator is that as you ascend through the multiple realms/worlds and elevate to where it once was, it will have already expanded beyond those previous boundaries, leaving you with the inner urge to continue reaching for the greater part of its divine self. Therefore, while you have an ability to reach a part of its divine presence, as it continues forward, the spiral of its breath gives you an everlasting existence of continuous desire to strive toward. Know that the Creator continues to create higher universes for you to attain, only to begin again. And then again. Consciousness is truly everlasting.

All of your angels on the other side are diligently working to help you through the ascension because they know Earth is the hardest place to graduate from. Know that this is the most glorious time to be present on Earth for self-growth and earning your place in this time of supreme ascension. The Eternal

One is allowing more and more angels to come through Earth's portals so you may receive messages of love, guidance and protection. All of this will help you awaken and return home.

Remember that there are worlds within worlds, systems within systems, universes within universes, and omniverses within omniverses. Everything spirals from the center of the Source and all worlds ascend in graduated order—something like a loving chain reaction.

Now let me give you a simplified illustration of this spiral of infinity and explain how the process of ascension continually evolves in unspeakable joy. **(See Illustration #14, next page)**

In this example I am giving you a simple drawing consisting of concentric circles that are an analogy representing the spiral of infinity, or the energy pattern by which ascension continues in its everlasting evolutionary process. There are no mathematics to adequately explain infinity but this drawing may suggest a process for your intellect to grasp. Please notice there are twelve bands representing twelve worlds leading into a thirteenth core at the center of the circle. This is an *inner* journey all beings must take so you might think of the bands or worlds as your own consciousness. In your Universe all ascensions begin at the outside perimeter at level one and *spiral inward* toward level thirteen. Presently you of Earth are about ready to enter into that first world from any of Earth's vortices, portals or doorways. Here you will be joined by other beings of advancing consciousness who are also ready to enter world one.

As you will observe in the illustration there are twelve triangular or pie-shaped sectors inside of world one. Each of these twelve sectors contains 12,000 dimensions. Each of the 12,000 dimensions holds a realm—so there are also 12,000 realms. Then within each of the 12,000 realms, each realm contains an angelic degree of glory, making a total of 12,000 angelic degrees of glory. The combination of all these categories totals 36,000 in one sector, which equates to the sacred

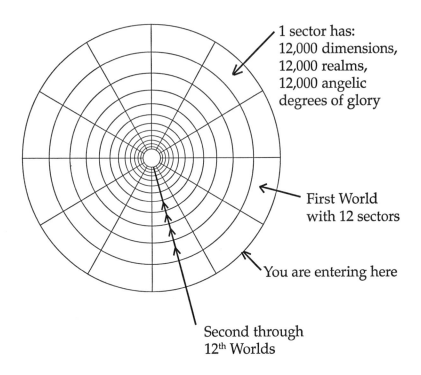

1 sector has:
12,000 dimensions,
12,000 realms,
12,000 angelic
degrees of glory

First World
with 12 sectors

You are entering here

Second through
12ᵗʰ Worlds

Illustration #14 - Circle of Oneness

number 9. Multiplying the twelve sectors times 36,000 equals 432,000 in the first world, which again equates to the sacred number 9. So, the 432,000 (which is the sacred number 9) represents a *limitless* invitation from universal light and love recreating itself. This allows *everyone* who chooses God to begin and advance through these twelve worlds of ascension at their own pace. It is all free will.

In the same way that you understand the first world/level notice that each of the other eleven worlds also has its own sectors, dimensions, realms, and angelic degrees of glory to be achieved. Progressing from levels one through twelve takes you into the thirteenth world, which is a bridge into another Universe. As your consciousness level progresses in the spiral of infinity you will one day earn passage into a new Universe with all the experiences and joy that it will contain.

VE: Wow. Those twelve worlds look a little intimidating. Have you any suggestions on how to be grateful for the struggles we go through that motivate us into our new life experiences en route to the thirteenth world?

AM: Struggle is a powerful energetic force that assists you in finding your way back home. Everyone is struggling to go back to the center (home) and to find joy and peace. In your world everything has a certain vibration of struggle—be it social struggle or inner struggle. The struggle of plants, animals and humans are merely the expression of this great eternal force. When you begin to let go and really work at living and bringing positive thinking and actions into your life, you will find that life will afford you more joy. The struggles then begin to lessen.

My suggestion is to start every morning as you awaken by thanking God for giving you another moment of breath. Continue to be grateful for your loved ones, family, and friends, and for your own gifts and talents. Through meditation/prayer say that you will awake this day to recognize your miracles and the experiences (positive or negative) that will come before you. Understand that this, too, is another kind of miracle for your awakening process.

Then at night, prior to sleep, think about what has happened and acknowledge how many miracles have been given you this day. As you continue to do this, your miracles will grow, and in this way you will advance and develop a positive attitude. Your struggles can change into miracles.

VE: Thank you so much for your willingness to guide our lives, beloved Archangel Michael. We appreciate and love you! Now please conclude the book with whatever advice and blessings you want us to have.

AM: There are many changes that are coming, but these are not negative although they may seem to appear that way. Don't fall prey to the illusion. I suggest that you center yourself through quiet contemplation and seek the kingdom within. Always ask for the divine light to guide you through your daily walk of life. By this centering process you can open the doors of higher knowledge that will give you the answers you seek. I am asking you to see yourselves as spiritual beings, because you are far greater than your human shell.

You are the souls of the living Oneness. The living breath of Oneness is ready to birth itself again (when the word is spoken) and many more worlds will be created through the finale of ascension. The most important aspect of living life, beloved ones, is to love God with all your heart, soul and mind. Love each other and know that your experiences through giving, accepting and being love are the only vibrations that harmonize with the tunnel of light that lifts you out of the earthly body for your celestial home.

Remember! What is happening upon your Earth is not negative—it is simply change and change is inevitable. As each day births itself before you, love it, and live it with compassion, fervor, and joy. Living the experience with a positive attitude will bring enlightenment. It is your choice as to what you decide to create, *but you do have three grand purposes in life—to love yourself—love others—and love what you do.*

There will be many changes and many signs in the heavens. Many of the celestial beings will be appearing throughout your skies and many of you will be seeing far more of these angelic messengers as time passes into your future. No longer can the existence of these celestials be denied by those in the seats of power, for humanity itself will be awakened, from city to city, state to state, and country to country.

My purpose in coming to the Earth plane is to teach the higher knowledge of Universal Truth and to transmute negativity. I seek to have you build centers of learning, to gather the enlightened, and to join the kindred souls together so each may unveil their wisdom, love and spiritual gifts. These will be the emissaries of the New Century who are learning and demonstrating strength in order to be able to endure the vibrational changes on Earth. These emissaries will be centered in light and will maintain self-mastery, self-attainment, and self-sovereignty in order to achieve ascension. Ask for the Father/Mother's will to go out before you and to make your way clear, for it is not your will but the will of God that is assisting you in fulfilling your destiny.

I ask that the Eternal Oneness take each of you into the depths of your being so that you may find the eternal Flower of Fire within you. May this infinite light enfold you and give you peace, wisdom and strength so that you can become a beacon of light transmuting negativity, demonstrating love, and bringing peace to humanity. Be assured we will unite once again as the portals of heaven open for the finale of Earth's ascension.

Know that I leave you now only through this written message, but of course we are never truly separated within the great circle of love and peace that continues eternally. Accept that you are truly blessed and are never alone. Then with that power and support be about the Father/Mother's plan on Earth.

So mote it be. May peace be ever with you. Until we come again, Adoni, Adoni, Vassu Barogas—which simply means that the essence of breath resides within the living temple and we are all one through the whole of creation. By way of the Creator we come to serve and to unite those who will be ready to join us within the eternal light of the higher worlds.

Products and Services

S.E.E. Publishing Company
>   books and audio tapes

Blue Rose Productions – Orpheus Phylos
>   soul messages, special consultations,
>   speaking engagements, angelic
>   geometrical nameplates, special projects,
>   travel excursions

ABR Audio Products – Tom Kenyon
>   books, audio and video tapes

Love Corps Network and Share Foundation
>   newsletter, network, soul readings,
>   counseling sessions

Order Form

Have you ever felt the stars were calling you? Here's your opportunity to find out why.

Irving Feurst, a soul clairvoyant able to see 17 of our 30 human subtle body fields, brings dramatic information for humanity's evolution. Irving and Virginia clarify:

• Why celestial initiations are now offered and the empowerment they can provide.

• The process of celestial "shakti."

• Ancient Earth Keepers and the grid system.

• The Seven Rays of Creation and Christ Consciousness.

• The transformation of your body's cellular water field.

ENERGY BLESSINGS
from the STARS
by Virginia Essene and Irving Feurst

This book provides an opportunity to receive energy initiations from spiritual masters in seven star systems.

ARCTURUS...offers you the blessing of *Hope* through which all things become possible

POLARIS...offers you the blessing of *Breath* to help release past limitations

PLEIADES...offers you the blessing of *Love* to safely open your heart chakra

VEGA...offers you the blessing of *Compassion* to use for yourself and others

BETELGEUSE...offers you the blessing of expanded *Soul Awareness*

RIGEL...offers you the blessing of wholeness from the *Integration of Matter with Spirit*

SIRIUS...offers you the blessing of amplified and glorified *Christ Consciousness*

Spiritual Education Endeavors Publishing Co.
1556 Halford Avenue #288, Santa Clara, CA 95051-2661, U.S.A.
(408) 245-5457

$14.95 paperback • 5.5 X 8.5 • 264 pages • ISBN 0-937147-29-X
Library of Congress Catalog Card Number 98-061252

TRANSFORM YOUR CELLULAR WATER FIELD

Extraordinary audio tape recorded by Irving Feurst to accelerate your spiritual transformation!

Water. We cannot live without it, yet how many of us really understand its remarkable physical and spiritual properties—and the even more remarkable properties of water in living cells? As explained in the <u>Energy Blessings from the Stars</u> book, the water in your cells is not the same as tap water. Your cellular water is really a liquid crystal and, as such, is capable of holding information and subtle energy. As we evolve spiritually, the subtle energy field surrounding our cellular water becomes ever more organized, continually increasing its ability to hold information and hold higher vibrational energy.

Side one is an explanation and exploration of the mysteries of water. Side two is a remarkable guided meditation that releases a shakti—a metaphysical or spiritual energy that behaves intelligently—to accelerate the naturally occurring transformation of the energy field around your body's cellular water. The result is an acceleration of your spiritual evolution because your subtle bodies will be able to hold more information, more energy and higher vibrational energies.

This tape is imprinted with actual transformative frequencies that cannot be duplicated. Using this tape will increase the ability of your subtle bodies to benefit from shakti—the shaktis used in the initiations described in the <u>Energy Blessings from the Stars</u> book—as well as those used in many common forms of energy work. It is also possible that using this tape may deepen your meditations.

 Spiritual Education Endeavors Publishing Company
1556 Halford Avenue #288, Santa Clara, CA 95051-2661 USA
(408) 245-5457

Single cassette tape T103 $12.95 60 minutes
Please use the order form on the next to last page.

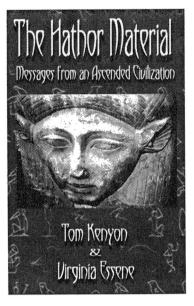

Did you know that the entire human race can be raised into a mass ascension experience? ...that photon energy could be used to raise our consciousness?... that alchemy may be closer than you think? What was the effect on our planet Earth of the comets' collision with Jupiter? Learn more about the true nature of time.

New Teachings for an Awakening Humanity, 1994/95 Revised Edition.

Here's an extraordinary book that has been highly recommended by Judith Skutch, A Course in Miracles; Eileen Caddy, Findhorn Community; and John Randolph Price, author. You will learn more about the true reason for Jesus' mission 2000 years ago and at the same time see a glimpse of the wondrous future that awaits us on Earth. "I come to advise you that humanity is not alone in the Universe...that your Earth is now being raised back into the higher love dimension she once held."— *The Christ*. The original text has been updated with over 50 pages of new information including two additional chapters titled the "Alchemy of Ascension" and "Your Natural Inheritance Reclaimed."

Virginia Essene, Editor

Spiritual Education Endeavors Publishing Company
1556 Halford Avenue #288, Santa Clara, CA 95051-2661 USA
(408) 245-5457

$9.95 paperback • 5.5 X 8.5 •264 pages • ISBN 0-937147-09-5
Library of Congress Catalog Card Number 94-068706

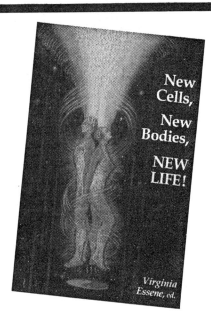

Blue Rose Productions

Presents
Orpheus Phylos

Dollye Ryan was anointed as Orpheus Phylos on January 22, 1984, by the Archangel Michael after surviving a near-death experience. The archangel made his presence known to Dollye in 1980, although he had been with her since birth.

BACKGROUND:

Orpheus, having studied metaphysics for the past thirty-five years and securing her Divinity Degree, has now established her own business, "Blue Rose Productions" in Mesa, Arizona. She has her Doctorate in Hypnotherapy from ARC in Costa Mesa, California. She plans to establish a center for the distribution of the Archangel Michael and the Celestials' teachings. This will be done through classes, lectures, tapes, literary works, home study and media.

COUNSELOR:

Orpheus counsels on an individual basis, using her mentor, The Archangel Michael. In each session Michael empowers you to love yourself and the Infinite One, to let go of separation and transmute fear into positive thinking and joy. Together they help you to find your inner direction for your desired success and spiritual development.

TEACHER:
Orpheus has taught thousands of people, using universal concepts of truth. Subjects covered are: the teaching and initiations of the Archangel Michael, mind development, numerology, science of symbols, meditation, telepathic writing, and communication techniques through color, light and sound.

LECTURER:
Orpheus is a dynamic speaker and audiences are entertained by the ease and lightness in which she works with her mentor, the Archangel Michael and her council of light. Orpheus is well acclaimed by the media, and is welcomed as a lecturer by religious and civic organizations, colleges, philosophical centers and numerous clubs and associations.

GOALS:
Orpheus' goal is to assist in the raising of consciousness and to bring more hope to humanity by teaching the universal laws. The greatest of these laws is to "know thyself" and in so doing you can only love and follow the divine presence within. The path through life is cluttered with emotional roadblocks stopping our spiritual growth and draining our daily energy. Yet we are all born with the ability to remove and overcome these obstacles and set a life course toward complete fulfillment.

* SERVICES *

SOUL MESSAGE – IN PERSON
This is a communicated message with the Archangel Michael through Orpheus. In this session you will be given a comprehensive overview of your soul's journey, encompassing past and present life experiences. This message helps to bring balance into ourselves and once "centered" we feel empowered to take decisive action in our lives. Many people have dramatically changed and greatly enhanced their lives through these sessions with Michael/Orpheus.
Rate: $125.00   60-75 minutes, taped

SOUL MESSAGE – BY PHONE
This is designed for those out of state that wish to have a spiritual message from the Archangel Michael/Orpheus. For

information read above!
Rate: $100.00   45-60 minutes, taped

SPECIAL CONSULTATIONS – IN PERSON OR BY PHONE

For those that are facing problems and needing spiritual guidance, consultations are as follows:

Rate: $25.00 - 15 minutes   Rate: $50.00 - 30 minutes
Rate: $75.00 - 45 minutes   Rate: $100.00 - 60 minutes.

TEACHINGS OF THE ARCHANGEL MICHAEL

Speaking and working through Orpheus, the Archangel Michael brings to Earth the transmutable blue flame to eliminate negativity. Michael teaches how to use the power of the inner worlds to accomplish a higher vibratory level thereby assisting those who are ready to attain self-mastery and to achieve alignment with the higher force of guidance. For those desirous of a rapid and comprehensive change in their life direction, Orpheus gives seminars in various locations. These seminars offer intensive studies, self-introspection and a spiritual clarity of one's own divine self.

ANGELIC GEOMETRICAL NAMEPLATES

You name projects an invisible array of beautiful geometrical activity patterns of color, light and sound. Every letter emits a color that depicts your mind abilities, skills, feelings and successes. This is a geometrical designed chart of your name and on the back of each chart is a written definition of the meaning of your name. The first name rules the mind, the second name rules the emotions, and the last name influences how you work in life. You can use these charts by relaxing and focusing your eyes on the arrays of color and allow your mind to receive inspiration, impressions and visions from your inner self. To see an example of name charts check Orpheus' web page.

Rate: $34.95 - 8½"x11" laminated chart (first name only).
Rate: $100.00 - 8½"x11" laminated charts (all three names).
Rate: $115.00 - 8½"x11" laminated charts (all three names +
                15 minute tape).

All products shipped will have a $3.50 s/h charge.

SPECIAL PROJECTS

This consultation is offered in giving assistance and information on issues pertaining to business affairs, construction and development projects and technological methodology.

Orpheus is always happy to create personalized programs to address these situations. Please contact her personally to discuss her innovative approaches and rates.

TRAVEL EXCURSIONS/CRUISES

Exciting trips offer opportunities to explore significant parts of our planet while studying with Orpheus and Michael and experiencing the major vortices. Please check Orpheus' web page for new events and trips planned for the upcoming future.

"OUT OF THE BLUE"

The "Out of the Blue" reports are channeled articles by the Archangel Michael and transcriptions from various lectures. These will be published by the Blue Rose Productions and will be designed to give a greater understanding of our lives and the world we live in today. The reports give insight, inspiration and hope to all those who read them.

INFORMATION

If you would like to be on Orpheus' mailing list, e-mail list, or if you want further information about her upcoming speaking engagements, seminars, classes, CD's, tapes, products, book sales and signing, please visit her web page or contact her at:

Orpheus Phylos
3370 N. Hayden Rd. #278
Scottsdale, AZ 85251
Phone: 480-775-4710
Cell Phone: 602-363-3385

-or-

E-mail: orpheus@blueroseproductions.com
Web Page: www.blueroseproductions.com

"Having trouble separating your delta waves from your thetas and super high Betas? Fear not: Tom Kenyon will help you get a grip on your consciousness, sub-consciousness, and altered consciousness in his book."

300 Pages • $11.95 Retail • ISBN 1-880698-04-9

Brain States—Kenyon, a psychologist and a musician, has spent years studying the effects of sound, music, and language on the human nervous system. Kenyon offers a technical excursion into how the brain works, noting the clear distinction between brain and mind. To do this he ascends to the heavens with Pegasus and drops by a shopping mall puddle to visit an amoeba. Through Kenyon's book, you will learn to overcome test anxiety, increase your intelligence, power your athletic abilities, hone your language skills, cure numerous psychological problems, tweak your creativity, and jump into altered states of consciousness.

AVAILABLE THROUGH: S.E.E. PUBLISHING

The Hathors' Self-Mastery Exercises on Audio Tape

The Self-Mastery Exercises in <u>The Hathor Material</u> book are also available on a convenient audio cassette tape. The tape was recorded by channel Tom Kenyon.

On this tape, Tom uses his remarkable four-octave vocal range, accompanied by the Tibetan bowl, to call the names of the archangels. This extraordinary sound called "toning" lifts one's subtle bodies into a high frequency state as a prelude to doing one or more of the Self-Mastery Exercises.

Tom guides the listener through each exercise and incorporates background psychoacoustic sound tracks to facilitate integration of the exercises. A special heart-opening meditation with the Hathors is also included!

Single cassette T102 $9.95.

Tom Kenyon's ABR Audio Products

In 1983 Tom Kenyon, M.A., formed Acoustic Brain Research (ABR) to scientifically document the effects of sound and music on human consciousness. As a psychological counselor and musician, Tom discovered that sound and music could be powerful catalysts for both personal growth and healing. By enrolling the efforts of numerous researchers in both private and university settings, ABR has substantially documented the positive benefits of psychoacoustic technology.

Since November 1997, S.E.E. Publishing Company has been distributing all of Tom's ABR tapes and compact discs. S.E.E. also sells Tom's book <u>Brain States</u>.

ABR tapes are remarkably successful in helping you achieve the self-enrichment and self-empowerment goals you seek. This is because of the scientific research, creative artistry, and advanced technology ABR invests in each program.

Music and sound have, from man's earliest cultures, been known to influence our states of mind. Now, through the application of advanced engineering, ABR utilizes the physics and psychology of sound to bring new scientific meaning and direction to this wondrous phenomenon.

ABR technology uses a variety of natural and electronic sounds, including specific sound patterns and frequencies,

Spiritual Education Endeavors Publishing Company
1556 Halford Avenue #288, Santa Clara, CA 95051-2661
USA (408) 245-5457

Tom Kenyon's ABR Audio Products continued . . .

differentiations of tone and vibration, synchronization, oscillations and pulsations, verbal and non-verbal input, tonal architecture, and hemispheric spanning. These are all orchestrated to stimulate the brain/mind into more resourceful states of awareness. Today, ABR is a recognized leader in psychoacoustic development and is acknowledged by professionals and lay persons alike as a source of the most advanced and neurologically-sound audio tapes available today.

BioPulse Technology™

ABR psychoacoustic technology is based on the use of complex tonal matrices in which various sound patterns are mixed to stimulate the brain/mind into more resourceful states. Many of these tones are mixed beneath the level of audible hearing, masked by other sounds, or sometimes music, specifically composed for the desired mental/emotional state.

ABR tapes and CD's also take advantage of "biopulse technology™" in which specific tones, known to affect brain states, are mixed into the tonal matrix. Research indicates that such frequencies can significantly alter awareness. These biopulse frequencies fall into a few broad categories, and a parenthetical note after each tape title/description indicates which biopulse frequencies are used.

The primary categories of the biopulse frequencies are:

Delta (0.5-4 Hz) - associated with deep levels of relaxation such as sleep

Theta (4-8 Hz) - associated with tranquil states of awareness in which vivid internal imagery often occurs

Alpha (8-12 Hz) - relaxed nervous system, ideal for stress management, accelerated learning, and mental imagery

Beta (12-30 Hz) - associated with waking/alert states of awareness

K-Complex (30-35 Hz) - clarity and sudden states of integration, the "ah-ha" experience

Super High Beta (35-150 Hz) - psychodynamic states of awareness

Spiritual Education Endeavors Publishing Company
1556 Halford Avenue #288, Santa Clara, CA 95051-2661
USA (408) 245-5457

AUDIO PRODUCT DESCRIPTIONS

Relaxation and Stress Management

Sound Bath
Soothe and relax yourself with this wonderful mix of beautiful music and ambient nature sounds. One of our most popular tapes for relaxation. (Theta range)
Single cassette T209 $13.95, compact disc CD209 $16.95

Wave Form
Wave Form gently "massages" your brain, helping you to dissolve tensions and drift into deeply relaxing states of awareness. (Theta range)
Single cassette T202 $13.95 *Headphones suggested.*

Wave Form II
Based on an ancient mantra believed to be the sound of the inner heart, this tonal matrix gently "opens the heart" thereby raising consciousness to a purer state of awareness, self-awareness and harmony. Beautiful vocals are intertwined with deep harmonic musical passages. (Theta range)
Single cassette T207 $13.95 *Headphones suggested.*

Rest and Relaxation (R & R)
For busy people who don't always get the rest they need, this tape includes *The 24-Minute Nap* and *The 22-Minute Vacation.* People love this tape! (Mid-Alpha to low Delta range)
Single cassette T402 $13.95 *Headphones suggested.*

Homage to Sol
Beautiful repetitive tempos for guitar, flute, and cello. Based on discoveries of the Lozamov Institute, this beautiful and restful music opens new vistas of serenity.
Single cassette T201 $13.95

Meditation

The Ghandarva Experience
A powerful journey into the spiritual realms of being. This unique program includes a 30-minute talk on the history of the Ghandarva and traces its roots back to Vedic India. Part Two is a compelling listening experience and includes the Chant of the Archangels and the Calling of Sacred Names, the Ghandarvic Choir, and a beautiful rendition of the 23rd Psalm.
Single cassette T801 $13.95, compact disc CD801 $16.95

AUDIO PRODUCT DESCRIPTIONS continued...

Singing Crystal Bowls

Ethereal sounds of quartz "singing crystal bowls" to enhance altered states of awareness. Stimulate your body's energy centers as the "crystal vibrations" flow throughout your body.
Single cassette T203 $13.95

New Video Tape Available

Sound Healing and the Inner Terrain of Consciousness. Tom explores the New Physics and its applications to Sound Healing. Part Two, **Song of the New Earth**, is a video collage of natural scenes from around the world. This visual experience has been mixed with a stereo sound-track of Tom's healing sounds. Approximately 60 minutes.
Video cassette(VCR)V101 $29.95

Fitness

The Zone

A delightful and truly effective tape designed to be used with a "Walkman-type" cassette player while doing aerobic exercises such as running, walking, etc. Increases your self motivation and encourages a more intense workout. (Alpha-Beta)
Single cassette tape T605 $13.95 *Headphones suggested.*

Self-Healing and Recovery

Psycho-Immunology

This widely acclaimed "self-healing" program helps you to explore the body/mind connection. It has been created to help you develop a greater potential for "healing experiences," and to assist you in your natural self-healing abilities. Note: Not a substitute for medical treatment. (Alpha-Delta)
Set of 3 tapes T401 $49.95 *Headphones suggested.*

Yoga for the Eyes

This tape offers eye movement exercises, guided imagery, and musical patterns to help rejuvenate your physically-strained and stress-weary sight. (Mid-Alpha range)
Single cassette tape T608 $13.95 *Stereo headphones required.*

Freedom To Be

Free yourself to make healthier decisions and live a fuller life. Designed as a recovery program for alcoholism and drug addiction, these tapes have been found to be very helpful with

issues of low self-esteem, self-sabotage, and emotional overwhelm. (Theta) *Headphones suggested.*
Two tape set with instructions T602 $29.95

Transformation Now!
A highly intense psychoacoustic stimulation of the brain/mind for rapid personal transformation. Note: Epileptics and persons with brain damage should not listen to this tape without professional help. (Shifts rapidly thru Alpha, Theta, and Delta)
Single cassette tape T302 $13.95 *Headphones suggested.*

Healing the Child Within
Unique guided imagery helps you to resolve deeply-held childhood issues. (Alpha to Theta range)
Single cassette tape T601 $13.95 *Headphones suggested.*

Mind/Brain Performance Increase

Creative Imaging
Processes used with this tape have been documented in independent tests to significantly improve analytical abilities, creative problem solving, learning, and insight. Protocols accompanying the tape can also be used to increase visualization abilities. (Mid-Alpha)
Single cassette T205 $13.95 *Headphones suggested.*

Mind Gymnastiks
This "flagship" of ABR's programs has been hailed by researchers, professionals, and laypersons as a highly innovative and powerful tool for helping to increase mental abilities and performance. Users report expanded creativity, speed of processing, perceptual clarity, and feelings of "being on top." (Low Delta to K-complex) *Stereo headphones required.*
Set of 6 tapes with instructions T700 $99.95

Inspired: High Genius and Creativity
Utilizing visual imagery and sophisticated archetypal psychology, these participatory tapes help you tap into the creative principles that great scientists and artists have used throughout history. Enter meditative states where enhanced visualization and inspired dreams help you gain insights into problem solving and goal attainment. (Mid-Alpha range) *Headphones suggested.*
Set of 4 cassette tapes with manual T701 $89.95

LOVE CORPS NETWORKING

The term *Love Corps* was coined in the book *New Teachings for an Awakening Humanity*. The Love Corps is a universal alliance of all human beings of good will who seek both inner personal peace and its planetary application. Thus the worldwide Love Corps family is committed to achieving inner peace through meditation and self-healing and to sharing that peace in groups where the unity of cooperation can be applied toward the preservation of all life.

In order to support our light-workers, wherever they may be, we publish the Love Corps Newsletter. Its purpose is to keep our Love Corps family informed of the very latest information being received from the Spiritual Hierarchy. Newsletter subscribers are eligible to join the Love Corps Network. Please send a SASE for an application.

Virginia Essene frequently travels around the United States and the world to link Love Corps energies, to share additional information not included in the books—*Energy Blessings from the Stars; The Hathor Material: Messages from an Ascended Civilization; You Are Becoming a Galactic Human; New Cells, New Bodies, New Life!; New Teachings for an Awakening Humanity;* and three other out-of-print titles—and to encourage humanity's achievement of peace and the preservation of all life upon planet earth.

Please contact us for further information if you would like to be involved in the Love Corps endeavors or to participate with us in seminars. Contact us to schedule a soul reading or an individual counseling session, in person or by telephone.

This "Time of Awakening" brings a new spiral of information to move each of us to a higher level of inner peace and planetary involvement. You are encouraged to accept the responsibility of this evolutionary opportunity and immediately unite efforts with other people in creating peaceful attitudes and conditions on our planet.

SHARE FOUNDATION
1556 Halford Ave. #288
Santa Clara, CA 95051-2661 USA
Tel. (408) 245-5457   FAX (408) 245-5460
E-mail: lovecorp@ix.netcom.com

Audio & Video Items (T = tape, CD = comp. disc, V = video)

Title	Code	Price	Qty	Title	Code	Price	Qty
Creative Imag.	T205	$13.95	___	Rest & Relax.	T402	$13.95	___
Freedom to Be	T602	$29.95	___	Singing C.B.	T203	$13.95	___
Ghandarva E.	T801	$13.95	___	Sound Bath	T209	$13.95	___
Healing . . .	T601	$13.95	___	The Zone	T605	$13.95	___
Homage to S.	T201	$13.95	___	Trans. Now!	T302	$13.95	___
Inspired: . . .	T701	$89.95	___	Wave Form	T202	$13.95	___
Mind Gymn.	T700	$99.95	___	Wave Form II	T207	$13.95	___
Psycho-Imm.	T401	$49.95	___	Yoga . . . Eyes	T608	$13.95	___

Transform Your Cellular Water Field	T103	$12.95	___
Hathors' Self-Mastery Exercises tape	T102	$ 9.95	___
Ghandarva Experience	CD801	$16.95	___
Sound Bath	CD209	$16.95	___
Sound Healing in the Inner Terrain of Consciousness with Tom Kenyon, video	V101	$29.95	___

Total of audio tapes, CD's, and videos (U.S. $) $_____ •

Books

Earth, the Cosmos and You .... @ $14.95	$_____	•
Energy Blessings from the Stars .... @ $14.95	$_____	•
The Hathor Material .... @ $12.95	$_____	•
New Cells, New Bodies, NEW LIFE! .... @ $11.95	$_____	•
New Teachings for an Awakening Humanity:		
English ed. (Revised 1994/1995) .... @ $9.95	$_____	•
Spanish ed. **Nuevas Ensenanzas** .... @ $5.00	$_____	•
Brain States by Tom Kenyon .... @ $11.95	$_____	•
Minus quantity discount (books only, see next page)	$(_____)	•

Product total (above items marked •)	$_____
Plus 8.25% **sales tax** (California residents only)............	$_____
Plus **shipping & handling** (see next page):................... (Amount is based on **Product total**, above)	$_____

Please send me the **Love Corps Newsletter:**

One year (bi-monthly) subscription = $24	$_____
Canadian & other international = $30 (airmail)	$_____
Earlier issues @ $4/issue U.S.A., $5 foreign. Specify year & mo. _____ J/F, M/A, M/J, J/A, S/O, N/D ..	$_____
Love Corps donation (tax deductible, see next page)	$_____

TOTAL ENCLOSED (add items within box) ....$_____

NOTE: Be sure to complete part 2 of the order form >>>>>>>>>

To: **S.E.E. PUBLISHING COMPANY**
c/o The SHARE FOUNDATION
1556 Halford Avenue #288
Santa Clara, CA 95051-2661 U.S.A.
Telephone (408) 245-5457   FAX (408) 245-5460
E-mail: lovecorp@ix.netcom.com (for info only)

Quantity discounts; books only:
 5 to 9 books - take off 10%
 10 or more books - take off 20%

U.S. Shipping & Handling Charges

Product total $	Amount	Product total $	Amount
$00.00 - $14.99	$3.95	$45.00 - $59.99	$8.45
$15.00 - $29.99	$5.45	$60.00 - $74.99	$9.95
$30.00 - $44.99	$6.95	$75.00 - $99.99	$11.45
		$100.00 and up	$12.95

Notes:
• Canada & Mexico add $2.00 to above Shipping amounts.

• Other International charges vary by country and weight; please call, FAX, or e-mail for rates.

• Please send check or money order in **U.S. funds** payable through a U.S. bank, or send an International money order made payable to S.E.E. Publishing Co. We **do not accept** foreign currency, or checks drawn on a foreign bank.

• We will ship your order by the best carrier. Some carriers do not deliver to P.O. boxes, so we must have both your street and postal address. Please request shipping rates for first class or air mail.
• All prices and shipping & handling charges are subject to change.

The Share Foundation is a non-profit organization. Contributions are tax deductible under section 501(c)(3) of the IRS code.

Please PRINT (this information is for your mailing label)

Name

Address

City   State/Province   Zip Code

(   )

Area Code   Telephone Number (optional)